CAMBRIDGE LIBRARY COLLECTION

Books of enduring scholarly value

History

The books reissued in this series include accounts of historical events and movements by eye-witnesses and contemporaries, as well as landmark studies that assembled significant source materials or developed new historiographical methods. The series includes work in social, political and military history on a wide range of periods and regions, giving modern scholars ready access to influential publications of the past.

The Revolution of America

First published in 1781, this work of the Abbé Raynal (1713–69) is the English translation of the last volume of his widely known and influential *Philosophical and Political History of the Settlements and Trade of the Europeans in the East and West Indies* which first appeared in 1770. Raynal's work begins a description of the distressed state of England in 1763 and her calls for help from the colonies in the build-up to the war. Written during the Revolution itself, the book speculates about the ending of the conflict in chapters entitled 'What ought to be the politics of the House of Bourbon, if victorious' and 'What idea should be formed of the thirteen united provinces'. Raynal's work was heavily criticised by, among others, Thomas Paine, who published *A Letter Addressed to the Abbé Raynal on the Affairs of North-America* (also reissued in this series) in 1782, correcting what he perceived as Raynal's mistakes and false assumptions.

Cambridge University Press has long been a pioneer in the reissuing of out-of-print titles from its own backlist, producing digital reprints of books that are still sought after by scholars and students but could not be reprinted economically using traditional technology. The Cambridge Library Collection extends this activity to a wider range of books which are still of importance to researchers and professionals, either for the source material they contain, or as landmarks in the history of their academic discipline.

Drawing from the world-renowned collections in the Cambridge University Library, and guided by the advice of experts in each subject area, Cambridge University Press is using state-of-the-art scanning machines in its own Printing House to capture the content of each book selected for inclusion. The files are processed to give a consistently clear, crisp image, and the books finished to the high quality standard for which the Press is recognised around the world. The latest print-on-demand technology ensures that the books will remain available indefinitely, and that orders for single or multiple copies can quickly be supplied.

The Cambridge Library Collection will bring back to life books of enduring scholarly value (including out-of-copyright works originally issued by other publishers) across a wide range of disciplines in the humanities and social sciences and in science and technology.

The Revolution
of America

Abbé Raynal

CAMBRIDGE UNIVERSITY PRESS

Cambridge, New York, Melbourne, Madrid, Cape Town,
Singapore, São Paolo, Delhi, Tokyo, Mexico City

Published in the United States of America by Cambridge University Press, New York

www.cambridge.org
Information on this title: www.cambridge.org/9781108031905

© in this compilation Cambridge University Press 2011

This edition first published 1781
This digitally printed version 2011

ISBN 978-1-108-03190-5 Paperback

T H E

R E V O L U T I O N

O F

A M E R I C A.

B Y

T H E A B B É R A Y N A L,

AUTHOR OF THE PHILOSOPHICAL AND POLITICAL
HISTORY OF THE ESTABLISHMENTS AND COM-
MERCE OF THE EUROPEANS IN BOTH THE INDIES.

L O N D O N:

PRINTED FOR LOCKYER DAVIS, HOLBORN.
MDCCLXXXI.

THE Philofophical and Political
Hiftory of the Eftablifhments and
Commerce of the Europeans; in
both the Indies, by the Abbé
RAYNAL, is certainly one of the
fineft works which have appeared
fince the revival of letters ; and
perhaps the moft inftructive of
any which have been known. It
is an original as to its formation ;
and ought to ferve henceforward
for a model. An additional part
to this work, difcuffing the difputes of Great Britain with her
Colonies, has been long and ar-
dently expected. In the courfe
of his travels, the tranflator happily fucceeded in obtaining a copy
of this exquifite little piece, which

A 2   has

has not yet made its appearance
from any prefs. He publifhes a
French edition, in favour of thofe
who will feel its eloquent reafoning
more forcibly in its native language, at the fame time with the
following tranflation of it; in
which he has been defirous, perhaps in vain, that all the warmth,
the grace, the ftrength, the dignity of the original, fhould not
be loft. And he flatters himfelf,
that the indulgence of the illuftrious hiftorian will not be wanting
to a man, who, of his own motion, has taken the liberty to
give this compofition to the public, only from a ftrong perfuafion,
that its momentous argument will
be ufeful, in a critical conjuncture,
to that country which he loves
with

with an ardour, that can be exceeded only by the nobler flame, which burns in the bofom of the philanthropic author, for the freedom and happinefs of all the countries upon earth.

It may not, perhaps, be quite needlefs to obferve, tho' it ought to be underftood, that the valuation of fums, made in the original in foreign money, is, in the tranflation, made in fterling.

The abundant good fenfe, the political fagacity, and even the falutary farcafm, to be found, amidft the effufions of benevolence, in this hiftorical tract, could never, it is apprehended, be more opportunely laid before thofe whom it may concern, than now. It now feems to be the general and anxious expectation, that, be-

A 3   fore

fore the rifing of Parliament from
its prefent feffion, fome proper
and efficacious fteps will at laft,
at this high time, be thought of,
towards clofing the unnatural, the
fhameful, and diftrefsful breach,
between the mother-country and
her colonies ; a breach in which,
as it is obferved, with great truth,
by the author of a Plan of Accommodation*, founded in juftice and
liberality, " The people on both
" fides are robbed of their trueft
" interefts, and made to facrifice
" their mutual happinefs, to gain
" nothing but contempt and mi-
" fery."

Let not Wifdom utter her
voice in the ftreets, and no man
regard her.

* Printed in 1780.

The

The Translator cannot help most solicitously wishing that some of his fellow-subjects, of the British dominions, may enter the lists for the prize proposed in the following Advertisement from the Academy of Lyons, in the hope that he shall have the happiness to see it borne from the rest of the lettered world, by a hero of that people, who have been dear, tam Marti quàm Mercurio, who are yet distinguished for their eloquence, and who, he trusts, when fraternal feuds shall be reconciled, will vindicate their superiority in arms. He humbly offers his service to any candidate for this prize, productive of so great celebrity, who may not know the ready means

A 4   of

of doing it himſelf, to get his performance conveyed to Lyons, free of poſtage, provided that it be left with his Bookſeller, Mr. Lockyer Davis, before the firſt of December, 1782.

London, March 5, 1781.

A D-

ADVERTISEMENT

FROM

THE ACADEMY

OF SCIENCES, POLITE LITERATURE, AND ARTS,

AT LYONS.

THE ABBE' RAYNAL, after having inſtructed mankind by his writings, would ſtill contribute to the improvement of their knowledge, by exciting emulation. An Aſſociate in the labours of the Academy of Lyons, he propoſed to it to give out two ſubjects for prizes, of which he has conſtituted the fund, to be diſtributed by the Academy, to the authors whom

whom it ſhall judge to have beſt anſwered the views of the propounded queſtions.

The Academy accepted of the offer with gratitude, and publiſhes the ſubjects without delay.

The firſt ſubject propoſed for the year 1782, relating excluſively to the manufactures and proſperity of the city of Lyons, is omitted here, as, however judicious and patriotic in the founder of the prize, it is an object only of particular concern, and, conſequently, not intereſting, like the ſecond, to the world at large.

FOR

[xi]

FOR THE YEAR 1783.

THE ACADEMY propofes the following fubject.

Has the difcovery of America been ufeful or hurtful to mankind?

If advantages have refulted from it, what are the means to preferve and increafe them?

If difadvantages, what are the means to remedy them?

The prize confifts of the fum of fifty *Louis d'or,* which will be remitted to the fuccefsful author, or his affigns.

CONDITIONS.

Any perfon of any nation may be a competitor for this prize, except titulary and veteran academicians. The affociates of academies will be admitted. The authors

thors muft not let themfelves be known, directly or indirectly; they will put fome line, or motto, at the head of their performance, which will be accompanied by a note fealed up, containing the fame line, or motto, with their names and places of abode.

The Academy, confidering the importance of the fubject, fets no limits to the length of the compofition, but only wifhes the author to write in French or Latin.

No work can be admitted after the firft of February, 1783. The Academy will proclaim the prize the fame year, in it's public affembly, after St. Lewis's day, or the 25th of Auguft.

The packets are to be fent to Lyons, free of poftage, directed to

M. La

[xiii]

M. La Tourrette, *Secretaire
perpétuel pour la claſſe des Sciences,
Rue Boiſſac* ; or to

M. de Bory, *Secretaire perpetuel
pour la claſſe des Belles-Lettres, Rue
Boiſſac* ; or to

M. Aime' de la Roche, *Impri-
meur-Libraire de l'Académie, mai-
ſon des halles de la Grenette.*

Signed,

La Tourrette,
Perpetual Secretary.

Lyons, Sept. 5, 1780.

The

The Reader is entreated to correct the following errors of the prefs, and to pardon fome inaccuracies and gallicifms, occafioned by the well meaning zeal, which hurried the tranflator to give this piece to his country with all poffible defpatch.

Page Line
13.—1. *for* happy people, *read* happinefs of the people.
54.—6. *for* whom, *read* which.
84.—8. *for* Form pleas, *read* Form plans.
89.—20. *for* began, *read* begin.

C O N-

[xv]

CONTENTS.

THE

THE
REVOLUTION
OF
AMERICA.

ENGLAND was juft difengaged from a long and bloody war, in which her fleets had difplayed the banner of victory in all feas; in which a dominion, already too vaft, was augmented by an immenfe acceffion of territory in both the Indies. This fplendid face of things might have an impofing air abroad; but the nation was reduced within to groan for its acquifitions and its triumphs. Overwhelmed with a debt of £148,000,000, which coft her an intereft of £4,959,000, fhe was fcarcely fufficient to the moft neceffary expences with the five millions eight hundred thoufand pounds which remained to her of her revenue; and this revenue, fo far from being capable of increafe, had no certain and affured confiftency.

B   Land

Land remained loaded with a higher tax than it ever had been in time of peace. New taxes had been laid on windows and on houfes. Thefe acts laid a heavy charge on all real eftate. Wine, plate, cards, dice, all that was regarded as an object of luxury, or amufement, paid more than could have been thought poffible. To reimburfe itfelf for the facrifice made to the prefervation of the public health, in the prohibition of fpirituous liquors, the treafury had recourfe to malt, beer, cyder, and all the ufual beverages of the people. The fea-ports difpatched nothing to foreign countries, and received nothing from them, but what was burthened cruelly with duties, on the import and the export. Raw materials and workmanfhip were rifen to fo high a price in Great Britain, that her merchants found themfelves fupplanted in countries where they had never before experienced a competition. The profits of her commerce, with all parts of the globe. amounted not annually to above two millions and a half; and. from this balance in her favour, there muft have been de-ducted

ducted a million and a half, paid in interest
to foreigners, on their capitals placed in
her public funds.

The springs of the state were strained.
All the muscles of the body-politic, expe-
riencing at once a violent tension, were in
some sort displaced. It was a critical moment. It was necessary to let the people
breathe. They could not be relieved by a
diminution of expence. That of the government was necessary, either to give value to conquests bought at the price of so
much treasure, at the price of so much
blood; or to restrain the house of Bourbon, angered by the humiliations of the
last war, and by the sacrifices of the last
peace. In default of other means, to fix
both the security of the present, and the
prosperity of the future, an idea was
formed of calling the colonies to the aid
of the mother-country. This view was
wise and just.

The members of a confederacy ought *England
calls her*
all, in proportion to the extent of their *colonies to*
powers, to contribute to its defence and *her aid.*
to its splendour, since it is by the public

power

power alone that each clafs can preferve
the intire and peaceable enjoyment of its
poffeffions. The indigent man has, without doubt, lefs intereft in it than the rich;
but he has the intereft of his quiet in the
firft inftance, and in the next, that of the
prefervation of the public wealth, which
he is called upon to partake of by his induftry. There is no principle of fociety
more evident; and yet no fault in politics
more common than its infraction. Whence
can arife this perpetual contradiction between the knowledge and the conduct of
thofe who govern? From the vice of the
legiflative power, which exaggerates the
maintenance of the public power, and
ufurps, for its fancies, a part of the funds
deftined to this maintenance. The gold of
the trader, and of the hufbandman, with
the fubfiftence of the poor, torn from them,
in the name of the ftate, in their fields and
their habitations, and proftituted in courts
to intereft and to vice, goes to fwell the
pomp of a fet of men who flatter, hate,
and corrupt their mafter; goes ultimately
into ftill viler hands, to pay the fcandal

and

and the ignominy of their pleafures. It
is prodigally fquandered in a faftuous fhew
of grandeur, the vain decoration of thofe
who cannot attain to real grandeur, and in
feftivities and entertainments, the refource
of impotent idlenefs, in the midft of the
cares and labours which the right government of an empire would demand. A portion of it, it is true, is given to the public
wants; but inattention, and incapacity, ap-
ply it without judgment, as without œconomy. Authority deceived, and which
will not condefcend even to make an effort
at being undeceived, fuffers an unjuft diftribution in the taxes, and a manner of ga-
thering them which is itfelf but an oppreffion more Then is every patriotic fentiment extinguifhed. A war is eftablifhed
between the prince and fubjects. They
who raife the revenues of the ftate appear
to be no other than the enemies of the citizen. He defends his fortune from taxation as he would defend it from invafion.
Whatever cunning can purloin from power
feems lawful gain; and the fubjects, corrupted by the government, make reprifals

on the mafter by whom they are pillaged.
They perceive not, that in this unequal
combat, they are themfelves dupes and
victims. The infatiable and ardent treafury, lefs fatisfied with what is given, than
irritated by what has been refufed, reaches
eagerly, with a hundred hands, after what
one alone has dared to divert from its gripe.
It joins the activity of power to that of
intereft. Vexations are multiplied, under
the fpecious name of chaftifement and juftice; and the monfter who beggars all thofe
whom he torments, thanks heaven devoutly
for the number of the criminals who have
been punifhed by him, and of the crimes
by which he is enriched. Happy the fovereign who fhould not difdain, for the
prevention of fo many abufes, to render
to his fubjects a faithful account of the employment of the fums he might exact! But
this fovereign has not yet appeared; and,
without doubt, he never will appear. The
debt, however, of the protected people,
towards the protector-ftate, is not a lefs
neceffary and facred tie; and no nation has
difowned it. The Englifh colonies in North

America

[7]

America had not given an example of it;
and never had the Britifh miniftry recourfe
to them without obtaining the fuccour it
folicited.

But this fuccour was granted in gifts,
and not in taxes; fince the conceffion of it
was preceded by free and public deliberations in the affemblies of each eftablifh-
ment. The mother-country had found
herfelf engaged in expenfive and cruel
wars. Tumultuous and enterprizing par-
liaments had difturbed her tranquillity.
She had fallen into the hands of minifters
corrupt and bold; unhappily difpofed to
raife the authority of the throne upon the
ruin of all the rights, and all the powers
of the people. And even revolutions had
taken place, before an attack upon a cuf-
tom, ftablifhed and ftrengthened by the
happy experience of two ages, had ever
once been dreamed of.

The colonies in the new world had been
accuftomed to regard this mode of furnifhing their contingent, in men and money,
as a right. Had this pretenfion been doubt-
ful, or erroneous, prudence would have

B 4   for-

forbidden its being too openly attacked.
The art of maintaining authority is a deli-
cate art, which requires more circumfpection than is generally thought. They who
govern are perhaps too much accuftomed
to hold men in contempt. They regard
them too much as flaves, fubdued and bent
down by nature, whilft they are only fo
from habit. If you lay on them a new
load, take care left they fhake it off with
fury and with intereft. Forget not that
the lever of power has no other fulcrum
than opinion; that the power of thofe
who govern is in reality but the power of
thofe who fuffer government. Remind not
people attentively occupied by their labours, or fleeping in their chains, to lift
up their eyes to truths too terrible for you;
and whilft they are obeying, bring not to
their remembrance their right to command. When the moment of this fearful
roufing fhall arrive; when they fhall have
thought in earneft that they are not made
for their magiftrates, but that their magiftrates are made for them; when they fhall
once have been able to bring themfelves
4   together,

together, to feel the communication of kindred minds, and to pronounce with a voice unanimous ; *We will not have this law ; this practice is offensive* ; medium is no more ; you will be conftrained, by an unavoidable alternative, either to punifh or to yield ; either to be tyrannical or weak; and your authority henceforth detefted or defpifed, whichever part it take, will have to chufe from the people but their open infolence, or their hidden hate.

The firft duty, therefore, of a wife adminiftration, is to manage the prevailing opinions in any country : for opinion is the property moft dear to man, dearer even than his life, and confequently much dearer than his wealth. A wife adminiftration may, without doubt, endeavour to rectify opinions by information, or to alter them by perfuafion, if they tend to the diminution of the public power. But it is not permitted to thwart them without neceffity ; and there never was any neceffity for rejecting the fyftem adopted by North America.

In effect, whether the different fettlements in this new world had been authorized,

rized, as they wished, to send representa-
tives to parliament, where they might have
deliberated with their fellow-citizens on
the necessities of the British empire at
large; or, whether they had continued to
examine within themselves what should be
the contribution which it was right for
them to make, no inconvenience could
have resulted from it to the treasury. In
one case, the voice of their delegated clai-
mants would have been drowned in that of
the majority; and these provinces would
have found themselves legally loaded with
such a portion of the burden as it should
be wished to make them bear. In the
other, the ministry, continuing to dispose
of the dignities, the employments, the
pensions, and even of the elections, would
have experienced no more resistance to its
will in that hemisphere than in this.

But the maxims consecrated by custom
in America were not founded in prejudice
alone. The pretensions of the colonists
rested on the nature of their charters, and
on the still more solid basis of that right of
every English subject, not to be taxed without

out confent, expreffed by himfelf or his
reprefentative. This right, which ought
to be that of every people, fince it is
founded on the eternal law of reafon, ori-
ginated fo far back as in the reign of the
firft Edward. From that epoch the Englifhman has never loft fight of it. In peace,
in war, under weak or wicked kings, in
flavifh or tumultuous times, it has been his
unremitted claim. Under the Tudors, this
Englifhman has been feen to give up fome
of his moft precious privileges, and, un-
refiftingly, to fubmit his neck to the axe of
tyrants; but never to renounce the right
of felf-taxation. It was in the defence of
it that he has fhed rivers of blood, that he
has punifhed or dethroned his kings. In
fhort, at the Revolution in 1688, this right
was folemnly acknowledged, by the celebrated act, in which liberty was feen to
trace, with the fame hand with which it
had driven out the royal defpot, the conditions of the contract between a nation
and the fovereign it had newly chofen.
This prerogative of a people, much more
facred, without all queftion, than fo many
imaginary

imaginary rights which fuperftition would fanctify in tyrants, was, with regard to England, at once both the inftrument and the rampart of her liberty. She thought, fhe felt, that it was the only barrier which could for ever limit defpotifm ; that the moment which ftrips a people of this privilege, condemns it to oppreffion ; and that the funds, raifed in appearance for its fecurity, are fooner or later fubfervient to its ruin. The Englifhman, in founding his colony, had carried with him thefe principles beyond the feas ; and the fame ideas had been tranfmitted to his progeny.

Ah ! if in the countries even of Europe, in which flavery feems long fince to have taken its feat in the midft of vices, of riches, and of arts ; in which the defpotifm of armies fupports the defpotifm of courts; in which man, chained from his cradle, and bound tightly by all the cords both of policy and fuperftition, has never breathed the air of liberty; if in thefe countries, notwithftanding, they who have once in their lives reflected on the fate of nations, cannot forbear adopting the max-ims,

ims, and envying the happy people who
knew how to make it the ground-work and
foundation of their conftitution; how much
more ought the Englifh natives of America
to be attached to the glorious birth-right
they inherit! They know the price at which
their anceftors had bought it. The very
foil which they inhabit muft produce in
them a fentiment favourable to thefe ideas.
Difperfed throughout an immenfe continent; free as the wild nature which furrounds them, amidft their rocks, their
mountains, the vaft plains of their deferts,
on the confines of thofe forefts in which all
is ftill in its favage ftate, and where there
are no traces of either the flavery or the
tyranny of man, they feem to receive from
every natural object a leffon of liberty and
independance. Befides, thefe people, given
up almoft all of them to agriculture and
to commerce, to ufeful labours which
elevate and fortify the foul in infpiring
fimple manners, hitherto as far removed
from riches as from poverty, cannot be
yet corrupted either by the excefs of luxury, or by the excefs of want. It is in
this

[14]

this ſtate above all others, that the man
who enjoys liberty is moſt capable to
maintain it, and to ſhew himſelf jealous
in the defence of an hereditary right,
which ſeems to be the moſt certain ſecu-
rity for all the reſt. Such was the reſo-
lution of the Americans.

*England
exacts from
her colonies
what ſhe
ſhould but
have re-
queſted.* Whether the Britiſh miniſtry were ignorant of theſe diſpoſitions, or whether they
hoped that their delegates would ſucceed
in changing them, they laid hold of the
moment of a glorious peace for exacting
a forced contribution from the colonies.
For war, and let it be well remarked, war,
whether unfortunate or ſuccefsful, ſerves
always as a pretext for the uſurpations of
governments; as if the directors of the
warring powers propoſed to themſelves by
it leſs to vanquiſh their enemies than to
euſlave their ſubjects. The year 1764 ſaw
the birth of the famous ſtamp-act, which
forbid the admiſſion in the courts of juſtice of any inſtrument which ſhould not
be written on paper marked and ſold for
the profit of the Britiſh treaſury.

The

The Englifh provinces of North America become indignant at this ufurpation, of their moft precious and moft facred rights. By an unanimous agreement they renounce the confumption of whatever was furnifhed them by the mother-country, 'till it fhould have withdrawn this illegal and oppreffive bill. Even the women, whofe weaknefs might have been feared, are the moft ardent, facrificing the fub-ferviencies to their drefs and ornament; and the men, animated by this example, give up on their part other conveniences and enjoyments. Many cultivators of land quit the plough, to form themfelves to the induftry of the workfhop; and wool, flax, and cotton, coarfely wrought, are fold at the price which would before have purchafed the fineft cloths and the moft beautiful ftuffs.

This kind of confpiracy ftuns the go-vernment. By the clamour of the mer-chants, whofe wares are without vent, its inquietude is encreafed. The enemies of the miniftry uphold thefe difcontents; and the ftamp-act is revoked after two

years

years of a convulfive agitation, which in other times would have lighted up a civil war.

But the triumph of the Colonies is of fhort duration. The parliament, which had retreated but with extreme repugnance, ordains, in 1767, that the revenue which could not be obtained by means of ftamps fhould be raifed by taxes on the glafs, the lead, the pafte-board, the colours, the paper-hangings, and the tea, which are carried from England to America. The people of the Northern Continent are not lefs revolted at this innovation than at the former. In vain are they told that no one could difpute the right of Great Britain to lay on her exportations the duties which her intereft demands, fince fhe denies not to her Colonies, fituated beyond the feas, the liberty of fabricating themfelves the wares fubjected to the new taxation. This fubterfuge appears but as a derifion to men, who, being cultivators of land alone, and reduced to the having no communication but with their mother country, cannot procure, either by their own induftry,

or

or by foreign connections, the objects which had recently been taxed. Whether this tribute be paid in the old or new world, they perceive that the word makes no alteration in the thing, and that their liberty would not be lefs attacked by this mode, than by that which had been repelled by them with fuccefs. The Coloniſts fee clearly that the government would beguile them; and they will not be beguiled. Thefe political fophifms appear to them as they are, the maſk of tyranny.

Nations in general are made more for feeling than for thinking. The greateſt part of them never had an idea of analyf- ing the nature of the power by which they are governed. They obey without reflec- tion, and becaufe they have the habit of obeying. The origin and the object of the firſt national aſſociations being un- known to them, all refiſtance to government appears to them a crime. It is chiefly in thofe ſtates where the principles of legiſ- lation are confounded with thofe of reli- gion, that this blindnefs is to be met with. The habit of believing favours the habit

C   of

of fuffering. Man renounces not any one object with impunity. It feems as if nature would revenge herfelf upon him who dares thus to degrade her. The fervile difpofition which fhe ftamps upon his foul in confequence, extends itfelf throughout. It makes a duty of refignation as of meannefs; and kiffing chains of all kinds with refpect, trembles to examine either its doctrines or its laws. In the fame manner that a fingle extravagance in religious opinions is fufficient to make many more to be adopted by minds once deceived, a firft ufurpation of government opens the door to all the reft. He who believes the greater, believes the lefs; he who can do the greater, can do the lefs. It is by this double abufe of credulity and authority that all the abfurdities in matters of religion and of policy have been introduced into the world for the harraffing and the crufhing of the human race. Thus at the firft fignal of liberty amongft nations, they have been prompted to fhake off both thefe yokes together; and the epoch in which the human mind began to difcufs

3   the

the abufes of the church and clergy, is
that in which reafon perceived at laft the
rights of men; and in which courage attempted to fet the firft limits to defpotic
power. The principles of toleration and
of liberty, eftablifhed in the Englifh colonies, had made them a different people
from all others. There it was known what
was the dignity of man; and when the
Britifh miniftry violated it, it could not be
otherwife but that a people all compofed
of denizens, fhould rife againft the wick-
ednefs of the attempt.

Three years elapfed, without a revenue
from any one of the taxes which had fo
wounded the Americans to the quick. This
was fomething : but it was not all to which
men jealous of their prerogatives had pretenfions. They infifted upon a general
and formal renunciation of what had been
fo illegally ordained ; and this fatisfaction
was given them in 1770. Tea only was
excepted. But the object of this exception was only to palliate the fhame of entirely giving up the fuperiority of the mother country over her colonies : for this

C 2   duty

duty was not more cogently exacted than the others had been.

The miniftry, deceived by their delegates, believed undoubtedly that the difpofition of the new-world was altered, when, in 1773, they ordered the collection of the duty upon tea.

At this news the indignation becomes general in North America. In fome provinces, formal thanks are agreed upon to be rendered to the mafters of veffels who would not fuffer this production to make any part of their cargo. In others, the merchants to whom it is configned will not receive it. Here, he is declared an enemy of his country who fhall dare to vend it. There, they are ftigmatized with the fame reproach who fhall keep it in their ftores. Many provinces folemnly renounce the ufe of this elegant refrefhment. A ftill greater number burn what they had remaining of this leaf, 'till then the object of their delight. The tea fent to this part of the globe was valued at more than two hundred thoufand pounds; and not a fingle cheft of it was landed. Bofton was the

principal

principal theatre of this infurrection. Its inhabitants deftroyed, in their very port, three cargoes of tea which arrived from Europe.

This great town had always appeared more occupied by a fenfe of its rights than the reft of America. The leaft attempt that was made upon their privileges had been repelled without fcruple and without referve. This refiftance, fometimes not unaccompanied by tumult, had for fome years been tirefome to government. The miniftry, who had a vengeance to wreak, feized too eagerly upon the circumftance of a blameable excefs; and required the parliament to punifh it feverely.

Moderate men wifhed that the offending town might be fentenced only to an in-demnification proportioned to the wafte that had been made in its road, and to fuch amends as it ought to make for not having punifhed this act of violence. This fen-tence was thought too flight; and on the 13th of March, 1774, a bill was paffed for fhutting up the port of Bofton, and forbidding any thing to be landed or loaded at it.

C 3   The

The court of London applauded itſelf for ſo rigorous a law, and doubted not but that it would bring the Boſtonians to that diſpoſition to ſlavery which it had vainly laboured 'till then to give them. If, contrary to all appearance, theſe ſturdy men ſhould perſevere in their pretenſions, their neighbours would be ardent in profiting from the interdiction laid upon the principal harbour of the province. Suppoſing the worſt, the other colonies, long ſince jealous of that of Maſſachuſet, would abandon it with indifference to its melancholy fate, and gather up the immenſe trade which would flow in to them on the tide of its misfortunes. By theſe means would be broken the union of theſe different eſtabliſhments, which had for ſome years paſt acquired a greater degree of conſiſtency than was pleaſing to the mother-country.

The expectation of the miniſtry was totally deceived. An act of rigour ſometimes over awes. The people who have murmured as long as the thunder-ſtorm growled only at a diſtance, when it comes

to

to burſt upon them frequently ſubmit. It
is then that they weigh the advantages and
diſadvantages of reſiſtance; that they con-
template their own ſtrength and that of
their oppreſſors; that a panic terror ſeizes
thoſe who have every thing to loſe, without
any thing to gain; that they lift up their
voice, that they intimidate, that they corrupt; that diviſion ariſes in the minds of
men, and that the community is ſeparated
into two factions, which irritate each other,
which come oftentimes to blows, and cut
each other's throats under the eyes of
their tyrants, who with ſweet complacency
behold their ſtreaming blood. But tyrants
ſeldom find accomplices but amongſt a
people already corrupted to their hands.
It is vice which gives them allies amongſt
thoſe whom they oppreſs. It is unmanly
ſoftneſs, which, filled with terrors, dares
not barter its repoſe for honourable peril.
It is the vile ambition to command, which
lends its arm to deſpotic power, and con-
ſents to be a ſlave in order to domineer;
to give up a people in order to partake
their ſpoil; and to renounce real honour

　　　　　for

for the obtaining of titles, the nick-names
of honour. It is, above all, the indifferent
and cold perfonality, which is the laft vice
amongft a people, the laft crime of governments, for it is ever the government which
gives it birth; it is that, which from
principle facrifices a nation to a man, and
the happinefs of an age and of pofterity to the enjoyment of a day and of a
moment. None of thefe vices, the production of a fociety opulent and voluptu-
ous, of a fociety grown old and verging to
its end, belong to a people newly eftablifhed and occupied in ufeful labours.
The Americans remained united. The
execution of a bill, which they called inhuman, barbarous, and bloody, tended but
to ftrengthen them in the refolution of
maintaining their rights with the more accord and conftancy.

At Bofton, the acrid and ardent fpirit is
more and more exalted. The cry of religion adds force to that of liberty. The
houfes of worfhip re-echo with the moft
violent exhortations againft England. It
was without doubt an interefting fpectacle
for

for philofophy, to fee that even in temples, at the foot of altars, where fuperftition has fo often bleffed the chains of nations, where priefts have fo often flattered
tyrants, liberty lifted up her voice in defence of the privileges of an oppreffed
people ; and if it can be thought that the
Deity vouchfafes to look down upon the
unhappy feuds of men, it was better pleafed
undoubtedly to fee its fanctuary confecrated
to this ufe, and hymns to liberty make a
part of the worfhip by which it was addreffed. Thefe exhortations of the preachers muft have had a great effect ; and when
a free people invokes heaven againft oppreffion, it delays not long to have recourfe to arms.

The other inhabitants of the province
of Maffachufet difdain even the idea of
drawing the leaft advantage from the difafters of the capital. They think but of
drawing clofer the bonds which unite them
with the Boftonians, difpofed rather to feek
a grave in the ruins of their common
country, than to let the leaft affault be
made

made on rights which they had learned to prize more highly than their lives.

All the provinces attach themſelves to the cauſe of Boſton; and their affection encreaſes in proportion to the ſufferings of this unhappy town. Nearly as culpable of a reſiſtance ſo ſeverely puniſhed, they are well aware that the mother-country but defers her vengeance againſt them; and that all the grace with which the moſt favoured can be flattered, is to be the laſt on which the hand of oppreſſion ſhall be doomed to fall.

Theſe diſpoſitions to a general inſurrection are augmented by the act againſt Boſton, which is ſeen circulating through-out the continent upon paper edged with black, emblematical of mourning for liberty departed. Soon the diſquietude communicates itſelf from houſe to houſe. The inhabitants aſſemble and converſe to-gether in the public places: and writings, full of eloquence and vigour, are delivered every where from the preſs.

" The ſeverities of the Britiſh Parlia-
" ment againſt Boſton (ſay they in theſe
" writings)

" writings) fhould caufe all the American
" provinces to tremble. They have now
" nothing left them but to chufe between
" fire and fword and the horrors of death,
" or the yoke of paffive, flavifh obedi-
" ence. Behold the æra of an important
" revolution is at length arrived, the event
" of which, as it fhall be happy or fuc-
" cefslefs, will claim and fix for ever
" either the regret or the admiration of
" pofterity.

" Shall we be freemen, or be flaves?
" On the folution of this grand problem
" is about to depend, for the prefent, the
" fate of three millions of men, and, for
" the future, the happinefs or mifery of
" their numberlefs defcendants.

" Awake then, roufe then, O Ameri-
" cans! Never did clouds fo black hang
" over the region you inhabit. You are
" called rebels, becaufe you will not be
" taxed but by your reprefentatives. Vin-
" dicate this juft pretenfion by your cou-
" rage, or feal the lofs of it with all your
" blood.

" Time

" Time for deliberation is no more.
" Whilſt the hand of the oppreſſor labours
" inceſſantly to forge your chains, ſilence
" would be guilt, inaction infamy. Let
" the preſervation of the rights of the
" commonweal be your ſupreme law.
" That man would be the laſt of ſlaves,
" who, in the danger into which the li-
" berty of America is fallen, would not
" exert every effort to preſerve it."

This diſpoſition was the common one :
but the important object, the difficult thing,
in the midſt of a general tumult, was to
contrive that a calm might be brought on,
by favour of which might be formed a concert of wills, to give dignity, ſtrength,
and conſiſtency to their reſolutions. It is
this concert, which, of a multitude of
ſcattered parts, and each eaſily to be
broken, compoſes a whole that is not to
be rendered tractable, unleſs it be to be
divided by policy or by power. The neceſſity of this grand combination, or totality, is ſtrikingly perceived by the provinces of New Hampſhire, of Maſſachuſet,
of Rhode-Iſland, of Connecticut, of New
York,

York, of New Jerfey, of the Delaware
counties, of Maryland, of Pennfylvania,
of Virginia, and of both the Carolinas.
Thefe twelve colonies, which were afterwards joined by Georgia, fent deputies to
Philadelphia, in the month of September
1774, charged with the defence of their
rights and interefts.

The difputes of the mother-country with
her colonies, affume at this period an importance to which they had not been before
intitled. It is no longer a few individuals
who make an obftinate refiftance to impe-
rious mafters. It is the ftruggle of one
body of men againft another; of the Congrefs of America againft the Parliament of
England; of a nation againft a nation. By
the refolutions taken on either fide, minds
mutually are heated. The ferment of ani-
mofity increafes. All hope of reconcilia-
tion vanifhes. On each fide the fword is
whetted. Great Britain fends troops to the
new world. This other hemifphere pre-
pares for its defence. Its citizens become
foldiers. The combuftibles are collected;
the conflagration is about to blaze.

Gage,

Gage, the commander of the royal
troops, fends from Bofton, in the night
of the 18th of April, 1775, a detachment
charged with the deftruction of a magazine
of arms, and other military ftores, collected by the Americans at Concord. This
body of troops meet at Lexington with
fome militia, whom they difperfe with
little difficulty, continue their march rapidly, and execute the commiffion to which
they had been appointed. But fcarcely are
they on their return towards the capital
but they find themfelves affailed, for the
fpace of fifteen miles, by a furious multitude, and death on each fide is given and
received. Englifh blood, fo often fhed in
Europe by Englifh hands, irrigates America in its turn, and the civil war is embarked in.

On the fame field of battle, the following months, more regular combats are be-
held. Warren becomes one of the victims
of thefe unnatural and murderous actions.
The Congrefs honour his afhes.

" He is not dead, (faid the orator) this
" excellent citizen fhall never die. His
" memory

" memory ſhall be for ever preſent, and
" for ever dear, to all good men, to all
" who love their country. In the ſhort
" ſpace of a life but of three and thirty
" years, he had diſplayed the talents of a
" ſtateſman, the virtues of a ſenator, the
" ſoul of a hero.

" Approach, all you whom the ſame
" intereſt inſpirits; approach your coun-
" tryman's ſtill bleeding body. Waſh
" with your tears his honourable wounds.
" But hang not too long over this inani-
" mated corſe. Return to your habitati-
" ons to fill them with deteſtation at the
" crime of tyranny. Let your horrible
" deſcriptions of it make each particular
" hair to ſtand on end upon your chil-
" dren's heads, inflame their eyes with
" noble rage, ſtamp menaces on their
" brows, and draw, by their mouths, indig-
" nation from their hearts ! Then, then,
" ſhall you give them arms ; and your laſt,
" your fondeſt wiſh ſhall be, that they
" may return victorious, or may die like
" Warren."

The

The difturbances by which the province of Maffachufet was agitated, were repeated in the other provinces. The fcenes, indeed, were not bloody, becaufe there were no Britifh troops ; but the Americans feize every where on the forts, the arms, and the military ftores ; they every where expel their governors, and the other agents of England ; and every where harrafs fuch of the inhabitants as appeared favourable to its caufe. Some enterprizing men have the fpirit even to take poffeffion of the works formerly errêted by the French upon the lake Champlain, between New England and Canada, and to make an irruption into this vaft region.

Whilft fimple individuals, or detached diftricts, are thus ufefully ferving the common caufe, the Congrefs is occupied with the care of affembling an army. The command of it is given to George Wafhington, a native of Virginia, and known by fome happy exploits in preceding wars. Inftantly the new general flies to the province of Maffachufet, drives the royal troops from poft to poft, and obliges them to fhut

I   themfelves

themfelves up in Bofton. Six thoufand of
thefe old foldiers, efcaped from the fword,
from ficknefs, from all the miferies incident
to their profeffion, and preffed by hunger,
or by the enemy, embark the 24th of
March 1776, with a precipitation which
partakes of flight. They go to feek an
afylum in Nova Scotia, which remained,
as well as Florida, faithful to its ancient
mafters.

This fuccefs was the firft ftep of Englifh
America towards the revolution. It was
begun to be openly defired. The principles which juftified it were difperfed on
all fides. Thefe principles, which were
indebted for their birth to Europe, and
particularly to England, had been tranf-
planted in America by philofophy. The
knowledge, and the difcoveries of the mother-country were turned againft herfelf,
and fhe was told that,

The colonies were in the right to feparate themfelves from their mother-country, independently of all difcontent.

Care muft be taken not to confound together fociety and government. That
they may be known diftinctly, their origin
fhould be confidered.

D   Man,

Man, thrown, as it were, by chance upon
this globe, furrounded by all the evils of
nature ; obliged continually to defend and
protect his life againft the ftorms and tem-
pefts of the air, againft the inundations of
water, againft the fire of volcanos, againft
the intemperature of frigid or torrid zones,
againft the fterility of the earth, which re-
fufes him aliment, or its baneful fecundity,
which makes poifons fpring up beneath his
feet ; in fhort, againft the claws and teeth
of favage beafts, who difpute with him his
habitation and his prey, and, attacking his
perfon, feem refolved to render themfelves
rulers of this globe, of which he thinks
himfelf to be the mafter : man in this
ftate, alone and abandoned to himfelf, could
do nothing for his prefervation. It was
neceffary, therefore, that he fhould unite
himfelf, and affociate with his like, in order to bring together their ftrength and intelligence in common ftock. It is by this
union that he has triumphed over fo many
evils, that he has fafhioned this globe to
his ufe, reftrained the rivers, fubjugated
the feas, infured his fubfiftence, conquered

a part

a part of the animals in obliging them to
ferve him, and driven others far from his
empire, to the depths of deferts or of
woods, where their number diminifhes from
age to age. What a man alone would not
have been able to effect, men have executed in concert; and all together they
preferve their work. Such is the origin,
fuch the advantage and the end of all
fociety.

Government owes its birth to the neceffity of preventing and repreffing the inju-
ries which the affociated individuals had
to fear from one another. It is the fenti-
nel who watches, in order that the common labours be not difturbed.

Thus fociety originates in the wants of
men, government in their vices. Society
tends always to good; government ought
always to tend to the repreffing of evil.
Society is the firft, it is in its origin independent and free; government was infti-
tuted for it, and is but its inftrument. It
is for one to command; it is for the other
to obey. Society created the public power;
government, which has received it from

fociety,

society, ought to confecrate it entirely to its ufe. In fhort, fociety is effentially good ; government, as is well known, may be, and is but too often evil.

It has been faid that we were all born equal ; that is not fo : that we had all the fame rights. I am ignorant of what are rights, where there is an inequality of talents, or of ftrength, and no fecurity nor fanction : that nature offered to us all the fame dwelling, and the fame refources ; that is not fo : that we were all endowed indifferently with the fame means of defence ; that is not fo : and I know not in what fenfe it can be true, that we all enjoy the fame qualities of mind and body.

There is amongft men an original inequality which nothing can remedy. It muft laft for ever ; and all that can be obtained by the beft legiflation, is, not to deftroy it, but to prevent the abufe of it.

But in making diftinctions between her children like a ftep-mother, in creating fome children ftrong and others weak, has not nature herfelf formed the germ or principle of tyranny ? I do not think it can

be

be denied; efpecially if we look back to
a time anterior to all legiflation, a time in
which man will be feen as paffionate and as
void of reafon as a brute.

What then have founders of nations,
what have legiflators propofed to themfelves? To obviate all the difafters arifing
from this germ when it is expanded, by a
fort of artificial equality, which might reduce all the members of a fociety, without
exception, under an impartial, fole authority. It is a fword which moves gently,
equably, and indifferently, over every head:
but this fword was ideal. It was neceffary
that there fhould be a hand, a corporeal
being who fhould hold it.

What has refulted thence? Why, that
the hiftory of civilized man is but the hiftory of his mifery. All the pages of it
are ftained with blood; fome with the blood
of the oppreffors, the others with the blood
of the oppreffed.

In this point of view, man appears more
wicked and more miferable than a beaft.
Different fpecies of beafts fubfift on different fpecies. But focieties of men have

never

never ceafed to attack each other. Even
in the fame fociety there is no condition
but devours and is devoured, whatever
may have been or are the forms of the government, or artificial equality, which have
been oppofed to the primitive and natural
inequality.

But are thefe forms of government, fuppofing them made by the choice, and the
free choice, of the firft fettlers in a country,
and whatever fanction they may have received, whether that of oaths, or of unanimous accord, or of their duration, are
they obligatory upon their defcendants ?
There is no fuch thing: and it is impoffible
that you Englifhmen, who have fucceffively
undergone fo many different revolutions in
your political conftitution, toffed as you
have been from monarchy to tyranny, from
tyranny to ariftocracy, from ariftocracy to
democracy, and from democracy to anarchy; it is impoffible that you, without ac-
cufing yourfelves of rebellion and of per-
jury, can think otherwife than I do.

We examine things with a philofophic
eye; and it is well known, that it is not

2   the

the speculations of philosophers which
bring on civil troubles. No subjects are
more patient than we are. I proceed then
in pursuit of my object, without any cause
to fear that mischief can follow from my
reasoning.

If the people are happy under their form
of government, they will keep it. If they
are unhappy, it will not be either your
opinions or mine, it will be the impossi-
bility of suffering more, and longer, which
will determine them to change it; a salu-
tary impulse, which the oppressor will call
revolt, though it be but the just exercise
of a natural and unalienable right of the
man who is oppressed, and even of the
man who is not oppressed.

A man wills and chuses for himself. He
cannot will nor chuse for another; and it
would be a madness to will and to chuse
for him who is yet unborn, for him who
will not yet exist for ages. There is no
individual but who, discontented with the
form of the government of his country,
may go elsewhere to seek a better. There
is no society but which has the same right

to change, as their anceftors had to adopt,
their form of government. Upon this
point, it is with focieties as if they were
at the firft moment of their civilization.
Without which there would be a great
evil; nay, the greateft of evils would be
without a remedy. Millions of men would
be condemned to mifery without end, Con-
clude then with me,

That there is no form of government
which has the prerogative to be immut-
able.

No political authority, which, created
yefterday, or a thoufand years ago, may
not be abrogated in ten years' time or to-
morrow.

No power, however refpectable, however facred, that is authorized to regard
the ftate as its property.

Whoever thinks otherwife is a flave. It
is to be an idolater of the work of his own
hands.

Whoever thinks otherwife is a madman,
who devotes himfelf to eternal mifery, who
devotes to it his family, his children, and
his childrens' children, in allowing to his

anceftors

anceftors the right of ftipulating for him
when he exifted not, and in arrogating to
himfelf the right of ftipulating for a progeny which does not yet exift.

All authority in this world has begun
either by the confent of the fubjects, or by
the power of the mafter. In both one and
the other cafe, it may juftly end. There
is no prefcription in favour of tyranny
againft liberty.

The truth of thefe principles is fo much
the more effential, becaufe that all power
by its very nature tends to defpotifm, even
in the moft jealous nations, even in yours,
ye Englifhmen, yes, in yours.

I have heard it faid by a whig, by a fa-
natic, if you will; but words of great
fenfe efcape fometimes from a madman;
I have heard it faid by him, that fo long as
the power fhould be wanting of taking to
Tyburn a bad king, or at leaft a bad minifter, with as little formality, preparation,
tumult, or furprize, as the obfcureft male-
factor is conducted thither, the nation
would not have either that juft idea, or that
full enjoyment, of their rights, which became

came a people who dared to think or to
fay that they were free; and yet an adminiftration, by your own acknowledgement,
ignorant, corrupted, and audacious, preci-
pitates you, with imperioufnefs and with
impunity, into the moft profound abyfs!

The quantity of your circulating cafh is
inconfiderable. You are overwhelmed with
paper; which you have under all forts of
denominations. Were all the gold of Europe collected in your treafury, it would
fcarcely pay the nation's debt. We know
not by what incredible illufion this ficti-
tious money is kept up. The moft frivo-
lous event might in the courfe of a day
throw it into difcredit. There is need but
of an alarm to bring on a fudden bank-
ruptcy. The dreadful confequences which
would follow this failure of faith, are beyond our imagination. And, behold, fuch
is the inftant marked out for you to make
you declare againft your colonies, that is,
to make you raife up againft yourfelves, an
unjuft, mad, ruinous war. What will become of you, when an important branch
of your commerce fhall be deftroyed;
when

when you fhall have but a third of your
poffeffions; when you fhall have maffacred
a million or two of your countrymen;
when your force fhall be exhaufted, your
traders ruined, your manufacturers reduced
to ftarve; when your debt fhall be augmented, and your revenue decreafed! Look
well to it; the blood of the Americans
will fooner or later fall heavy on your
heads. Its effufion will be revenged by
your own hands; and you are arriving at
the point.

But, fay you, *thefe people are rebels*——
Rebels! And why? becaufe they will not
be your flaves. A people fubjected to the
will of another people, who can difpofe as
they chufe of their government, of their
laws, and of their trade; tax them at their
pleafure; fet bounds to their induftry, and
enchain it by arbitrary prohibitions, are
bond-fervants, yes, certainly are bond-fervants; and their fervitude is worfe than
what they would undergo if governed by
a tyrant. Deliverance from the oppreffion
of a tyrant is effected by his expulfion, or
his death. You have delivered yourfelves

by

by each of thefe methods. But a nation is not to be put to death, is not to be ex-pelled. Liberty is only to be expected from a rupture, which by its confequences involves one of the nations, and fometimes both of them, in ruin. A tyrant is a monfter with a fingle head, which may be ftruck off at a fingle blow. A tyrannic nation is an hydra with a thoufand heads, for the cutting off of which a thoufand fwords muft be lifted up together. The crime of oppreffion committed by a ty-rant collects all the indignation upon him alone. The commiffion of the fame crime by a numerous fociety, fcatters the hor-rour and the fhame of it upon a multi-tude, which never blufhes. It is every body's fault and nobody's; and the refent-ment of injury wanders wildly in defpair, without knowing where to fix, or whither it is carried.

But they are our fubjects——Your fub-jects! no more than the inhabitants of Wales are fubjects to thofe of Lancafhire. The authority of one nation over another cannot be founded but upon conqueft,

upon

upon general confent, or upon conditions propofed on one part, and accepted on the other. Conqueft binds no more than theft: the confent of anceftors cannot be obligatory upon defcendants: and there can be no condition which muft not be underftood to be exclufive of the facrifice of liberty. Liberty is not to be bartered for any thing, becaufe there is not any thing which is of a comparable price. Such have been the difcourfes held by you to your tyrants, fuch hold we to you for your colonifts.

The earth which they occupy is our's——— Your's! it is thus you call it becaufe you ufurped it. But be it fo. Does not the charter of conceffion oblige you to treat the Americans as countrymen? Do you do fo? But we are well employed here truly in talking of conceffions by charters, by which men grant what they are not mafters of, what confequently they have not the right to grant to a handful of weak people, forced by circumftances to receive as a gratification that which belongs to them of natural right. And then, have

have the defcendants who are now living been called to a compact figned by their anceftors ? Either confefs the truth of this principle, or recall the defcendants of James. What right had you to drive him away which we have not to feparate our-felves from you ? fay the Americans to you : and what have you to fay in anfwer ?

They are ungrateful, we are their founders; we have been their defenders; we have run in debt upon their account——Say, as much or more upon your own than theirs. If you have undertaken their defence, it was as you would have undertaken that of the Sultan of Conftantinople, had your ambi-tion or your intereft required it. But have they not requited you, in delivering up to you their productions ; in receiving your merchandize exclufively at the exorbitant price you would pleafe to put upon it; in fubjecting themfelves to prohibitions which cramped their induftry, and to reftrictions by which you have oppreffed their pro-perty ? Have they not helped you ? Have they not run in debt upon your ac-count ? Have they not taken arms and

fought

fought for you? When you have made
your requests to them, which is the proper
way of dealing with freemen, have they
not complied with them? When did you
ever experience a refusal from them, but
when you clapped a bayonet to their breast,
and said, *Your money or life; die or be
slaves?* What! because you have been
beneficent, have you a right to be oppres-
sive? What! and shall nations too build
on gratitude the barbarous claim, to de-
base, and trample under foot, those who
have had the misfortune to receive their
favours? Ah! individuals perhaps, though
it is by no means a duty, individuals may,
perhaps, in a benefactor tolerate a tyrant.
In them, it is great, it is magnanimous,
undoubtedly, to consent to be wretched,
that they may not be ungrateful. But nations have a different morality. The pub_
lic happiness is the first law, as the first
duty. The first obligation of these great
bodies is with themselves. They owe,
before all other things, liberty and justice
to the members which compose them.
Every child which is born to the state,
every

every new citizen who comes to breathe
the air of the country he has chofen, or nature given him, is intitled to the greateft
happinefs he can enjoy. Every obligation
which cannot be reconciled with that, is
broken. Every contrary claim, is a wicked attempt upon his rights. And what
is it to him, that his anceftors have been
relieved, if he is deftined to be himfelf
oppreffed? With what right can be exacted from him the payment of this ufu-
rious debt of benefits, which he has never
felt? No, no. The wifhing to arm one's
felf with fuch a claim, againft a whole
nation, and its pofterity, is to overthrow
all the ideas of policy and order, and,
whilft one invokes the name of morality,
to betray all its laws. What have you
not done for Hanover? Do you command
at Hanover? All the republics of Greece
were bound together by mutual fervices;
but did any one exact, as a mark of
gratitude, the right of difpofing of the
government of the fuccoured ftate?

Our honour is engaged——Say, that of
your bad minifters, and not your's. In
what

what confifts the true honour of him who
has been miftaken ? Is it to perfift in his
error, or to acknowledge it ? Has he who
returns to a fenfe of juftice, any caufe to
blufh ? Englifhmen, you have been too
hafty. Why did you not wait, till the
Americans had been corrupted, as you are,
by riches ? Then, they would have thought
no more highly of their liberty, than you
do of your own. Then it would have
been needlefs to take arms, againft men
fubdued by opulence. But what inftant
have you chofen for attacking them ?
That in which what they had to lofe, their
liberty, could not be balanced by what
they had to keep.

But later they would be more nume-
rous——I agree, they would. What
then have you attempted ? the enflaving a
people who fhall be unfettered in fpite of
you by time. In twenty, in thirty years,
the remembrance of your atrocious deeds
will ftill be frefh ; and the fruit of them
will be ravifhed from you. Then, there
will remain to you but remorfe and fhame.
There is a decree of nature which you

E fhall

fhall not change; which is, that great
bodies give laws to little ones. But,
tell me, if the Americans fhould then un-
dertake againft Great Britain, what you
have now undertaken againft them, what
would you fay? Precifely what they at
this moment fay to you. Why fhould
motives which affect you fo little in their
mouths, appear to you more folid in your
own?

*They will not obey our parliament, nor
adopt our ordinances*——Did they make
them? Can they change them?

*We obey them readily enough, without hav-
ing had, in time paft, or having in the
prefent, any influence over them*——That is
to fay, that you are flaves; and that you
cannot bear that men fhould be free.
However, do not confound the fituation of
the Americans with your own. You have
reprefentatives, and they have not. You
have voices which fpeak for you, and no
perfon ftipulates for them. If indeed thefe
voices are bought and fold, it is an excellent reafon for their difdaining fuch a fri-
volous advantage.

They

They wish to be independent of us——Are not you so of them?

They will never be able to support themselves without us——If that be so, be quiet. Necessity will bring them back.

And if we should not be able to subsist without them——It would be a great misfortune: but to cut their throats in order to get out of it, is a singular expedient.

It is for their interest, it is for their good, that we are severe with them, as one is severe with frantic children——Their interest! Their good! And who made you judges of these two objects which so nearly touch them, and which they should better know than you? If it should happen, that a man should make a forcible entry into another's house, because, forsooth, he is a man of great sense, and nobody more able to maintain peace and good order for his neighbour, should not one be in the right to humbly beg he would be pleased to take himself away, and to trouble his head about his own affairs? And if the affairs of this officious hypocrite should be very badly ordered? If he should be at the

E 2   bottom

bottom but an ambitious mortal, who, under the pretence of settling and ordering, should have a violent inclination to usurp? If he should cover with the mask of benevolence, but views full of injustice, such, for example, as to get himself out of straits and difficulties at his neighbour's cost?

We are the mother-country——What, always the most holy names to serve as a veil to interest and ambition! The mother-country Fulfill the duties of it then. Besides, colonies are formed of different nations, amongst which some will grant, others refuse you this appellation; and all will with one voice tell you, There is a time when the authority of parents over their children ceases; and this time is when the children are able to provide for themselves. What term have you fixed for our emancipation? Be candid, and you will allow that you had promised yourselves to be able to hold us in a wardship or minority which should never end. If, indeed, this wardship were not to have turned for us into an insupportable constraint; if our

advantage

advantage were not for ever to be facrificed
to yours; if we were not to have had a multitude of thofe minor oppreffions, which, together, fwell to a bulk moft burdenfome, to
bear from the governors, the judges, the
collectors, and the military, whom you fend
us; if the greateft part of them, at their ar-
rival in our climate, were not to have brought
with them, blafted characters, ruined fortunes, rapacious hands, and the infolence
of fubaltern tyrants, who, tired, in their
own country, with obeying laws, come to
requite themfelves, in a new world, by
the exercife of an arbitrary power. You
are the mother country : but fo far from
encouraging, you fear our progrefs, bind
our hands, and reprefs and ftrangle our
growing ftrength. Nature in favouring us
deceives your fecret wifhes; or rather, you
would chufe, that we fhould remain in an
eternal childhood, with regard to all that
can be ufeful to ourfelves, and that, notwithftanding, we fhould be robuft vaffals,
to be employed in your fervice, and in
the furnifhing, without remiffion, new
fources of riches to your infatiable avidity.

Is

Is it this then to be a mother? Is it this to be a country to her children? Ah, in the forefts which furround us, nature has given a gentler inftinct to the favage beaft, which, become a mother, devours not at leaft thofe whom fhe has produced.

Were all their pretenfions to be acquiefced in, they would foon be happier than we are. And why not? If you are corrupted, is it neceffary that they muft be corrupted too? If you have a difpofition to flavery, muft they too follow your example? If they had you for mafters, why fhould you not confer the property of their country upon another power, upon your fovereign? Why fhould you not render him their defpot, as you have by a folemn act declared him the defpot of Canada? Would it then be neceffary that they fhould ratify this extravagant conceffion? And even if they fhould have ratified it, muft they obey the fovereign whom you fhould have given them, and, if he commanded it, take arms againft you? The King of England has a negative power. No law can be promulgated without his confent. Why fhould the

the Americans grant him, in their country,
a power, of the inconvenience of which
you are continually made fenfible? Should
it be, in order one day to diveft him of it,
fword in hand, as it will happen to you,
if your government be perfected? What
advantage do you find in fubjecting them
to a vicious conftitution?

*Vicious or not, this is our conftitution; and
it ought to be generally acknowledged and received, by all who bear the Englifh name;
without which, each of our provinces governing itfelf in its own way, having its own
laws, and pretending to independance, we
ceafe to form a national body, and are no
more than a heap of little republics, detached,
divided, continually rifing againft one another,
and eafily to be ufurped by a common enemy.
The adroit and powerful Philip, capable of
attempting fuch an enterprize, is at our door.*

If he is at your door, he is far from the
Americans. A privilege which may have
fome inconvenience with regard to you, is
not the lefs a privilege. But feparated, as
they are, from Great Britain by immenfe
feas, of what importance is it to you,

E 4   whether

whether your colonies receive, or reject,
your constitution? What does that make,
for, or against, your power; for, or against,
your safety? This unity, of which you
exaggerate the advantages, is still but a
vain pretext. You object your laws to
your colonies, when they are harrassed
by them; and you tread them under foot,
when they make in their favour. You tax
yourselves, and you would tax them. If
the least attempt is made upon this privilege, you make a furious outcry, fly to
arms, and are ready to run on swords in its
defence; and yet, you hold a dagger to
the breast of your countryman, to oblige
him to renounce it. Your ports are open
to all the world; and you shut up the ports
of your colonists. Your merchandize is
wafted where you please; and theirs must
necessarily come to you. You manufac-
ture, and you will not suffer them to ma-
nufacture. They have skins, they have
iron; and they must deliver up to you,
unwrought, this iron and these skins. What
you acquire at a low price, they must buy
of you at the price which your rapacity
impofes.

impofes. You offer them up as victims to
your traders; and becaufe your India
Company was in danger, the Americans
muft needs repair their loffes. And yet
you call them your countrymen and fellow-
citizens; and it is thus that you invite them
to receive your conftitution. Go to, go
to. This unity, this league which feems
fo neceffary to you, is but that of the filly
animals in the fable, amongft which you
have referved to yourfelves the lion's part.

Perhaps you have not fuffered yourfelves
to be drawn to the filling the new world
with blood and devaftation but by a falfe
point of honour. We wifh to perfuade
ourfelves that fo many crimes have not
been the confequences of a project delibe-
rately formed. You had been told, that
the Americans were but a vile herd of
cowards, whom the leaft threat would
bring, terrified and trembling, to acquiefce
in whatever it fhould pleafe you to exact.
Inftead of the cowards which had been de-
feribed and promifed you, you find true
men, true Englifhmen, countrymen worthy of yourfelves. Is this a reafon for
your

your being irritated? What! your anceftors admired the Hollander fhaking off the
Spanifh yoke; and fhould you, their de-
feendants, be angry or furprized, that your
countrymen, your brethren, that they who
feel your blood circulate in their veins,
fhould rather pour it on the ground and
die, than live in yokes and bondage? A
ftranger, upon whom you fhould have
formed the fame pretenfions, would have
difarmed you, if, fhewing you his naked,
breaft, he had faid, *Plunge in your poignard
here, or leave me free:* and yet you ftab
your brother; and you ftab him without
remorfe, becaufe he is your brother! Englifhmen! what can be more ignominious
than the favagenefs of a man,, proud of
his own liberty, and wickedly attempting
to deftroy the liberty of another! Would
you have us believe, that the greateft enemy to freedom is the man that is free?
Alas! we are but too much inclined to it.
Enemies of kings, you have their arrogance
and pride. Enemies of royal prerogative,
you carry it every where. Every where
you fhew yourfelves tyrants. Well then,

tyrants

tyrants of nations, and of your colonies, if in the event you prove the ftrongeft, it will be becaufe heaven is deaf to the prayers which are directed to it from all the countries upon earth.

Since the feas have not fwallowed up your bluftering ruffians, tell me, what will become of them, if there fhould arife in the new world a man of eloquence, promifing eternal happinefs to the martyrs of liberty who die in arms. Americans! let your preachers be feen inceffantly in their pulpits, with crowns of glory in their hands, pointing to heaven open. Priefts of the new world, now is the time for it; expiate the deteftable fanaticifm, which once laid wafte America, by the happy fanaticifm, begotten by policy upon freedom. No; you will not deceive your countrymen. To God, who is the principle of juftice and of order, tyrants are abomination. God has imprinted on the heart of man this facred love of liberty; he wills not that flavery disfigure and debafe his nobleft work. If deification be due to man, it is, undoubtedly, to that man who fights and dies

for

for his native foil. Put his image in your
temples; fet it on your altars. It fhall be
worfhiped by his country. Form a political and religious calendar, marking
each day by the name of fome hero, who
fhall have fpilled his blood to fet you free.
Your pofterity fhall one day read them
with holy joy: thefe, fhall it fay, behold,
thefe were the men who gave liberty to half
a world; and who, charging themfelves
with our happinefs, before we had exift-
ence, fecured our infant flumbers from the
being difturbed and terrified by the clank
of chains.

What was
the part
which Eng-
land fhould
have taken,
when fhe
faw the fer-
mentation
of her colo-
nies.

When the caufe of your colonies was
argued in your houfes of parliament, we
heard fome excellent pleadings pronounced
in their favour. But that which fhould
have been addreffed to you perhaps is
this:

“ I fhall not talk to you, my lords and
“ gentlemen, of the juftice or injuftice of
“ your pretenfions. I am not fuch a ftran-
“ ger to public affairs as not to know that
“ this preliminary difcuffion, fo facred in
“ all the other circumftances of life, would
“ be

" be mifplaced and ridiculous in this. I
" fhall not examine what hope you can
" have of fucceeding, or if you are likely
" to prove the ftrongeft in the event, tho'
" this fubject might, perhaps, appear to
" you of fome importance, and might,
" probably, infure me the honour of your
" attention. I will do more. I fhall not
" compare the advantages of your fitua-
" tion, if you fucceed, with the confe-
" quences which will follow, if you are
" unfortunate. I fhall not afk you how
" long you are determined to ferve the
" caufe of your enemies. But I will fup-
" pofe at once, that you have reduced
" your colonies to the degree of fervitude
" which you have authoritatively required.
" Shew me only how you will fix and keep
" them. By a ftanding army? But will
" this army, which will drain you of men
" and money, keep pace, or not keep
" pace, with the increafe of population?
" There are but two anfwers to my quef-
" tion; and, of thefe two anfwers, one
" feems to be abfurd, and the other brings
" you back to the po nt at which you are.
" I have

" I have reflected on it well; and I have
" difcovered, if I am not miftaken, the
" only rational and certain plan which you
" have to follow. And it is, as foon as
" you fhall be the mafters. to ftop
" the progrefs of population, fince it ap-
" pears to you more advantageous, more
" honourable, and more becoming, to
" domineer over a fmall number of flaves,
" than to have a nation of freemen for
" your equals and your friends.

" But you will afk me, how is the pro-
" grefs of population to be ftopped ? The
" expedient might revolt weak minds, and
" cowardly fouls; but happily there are
" not any fuch in this auguft affembly. It
" is, to ftab without pity the greateft part
" of thefe vile rebels, and to reduce the
" reft of them to the condition of the ne-
" groes. The high-fpirited and generous
" Spartans, fo extolled in ancient and mo-
" dern ftory, have fet you the example.
" Like them, and with their faces muffled
" in their cloaks, fhall our fellow-citizens,
" and the bravoes in our pay, go clandef-
" tinely, and by night, to maffacre the
" children

" children of our Helots, at their fathers'
" fide, and on their mothers' breaft; and
" leave alive but fuch a number of them,
" as may be fufficient for their labours,
" and confiftent with our fafety."

Englifhmen! you fhudder at this horrible
propofition, and you afk what part there is
to take. Vanquifhers, or vanquifhed, fee
here then what you ought to do. If the
refentment, excited by your cruelties, can
be calmed; if the Americans can fhut their
eyes to the devaftation which furrounds
them; if, in paffing over the ruins of their
towns deftroyed by fire, and their fields
whitened by the bones of murdered rela-
tives; if, in drawing-in with every refpi-
ration the fcent of the blood which your
hands have on all fides fhed, they can forget the outrages of your defpotifm; if they
can prevail upon themfelves to place the
leaft confidence in your declarations of con-
trition, and to believe that you have indeed
renounced the injuftice of your pretenfions,
begin by recalling your mercenary cut-
throats. Reftore freedom to their ports,
which you keep fhut up; withdraw your
                              fquadrons

fquadrons from their coafts ; and, if there
be a wife citizen amongft you, let him take
the olive-branch in his hand, prefent himfelf, and fay,

" O you, our countrymen, and our old
" friends; allow us this title; we have
" profaned it, but our repentance renders
" us worthy to refume it, and we afpire
" henceforward at the glory to preferve it.
" We confefs, in the prefence of this hea-
" ven, and of this earth, which have been
" confcious of it, we confefs, that our
" pretenfions have been unjuft, our con-
" duct has been cruel. Let it on each
" fide be forgotten. Raife up again your
" fortreffes and your ramparts. Reaffemble
" in your peaceable habitations. Let us
" wafh out the remembrance of every drop
" of blood that has been fpilled. We ad-
" mire the generous fpirit by which you
" have been directed. It is the fame with
" that to which, in fimilar circumftances,
" we have been indebted for our political
" falvation. Yes, it is by thefe marks,
" exprefsly, that we now know you to be
" indeed our countrymen, to be indeed
" our

" our brothers; concerning whom we have
" verily been guilty; and therefore is this
" diſtreſs come upon us. You would be
" free; be ye free. Be ſo, in the whole
" extent which we have ourſelves given to
" this ſacred name. It is not of us that
" you hold this right. Not unto us, not
" unto us, doth belong the power, by
" which it is to be given, or taken away.
" You have received it, as we did, from
" nature, which the ſins and ſwords of ty-
" rants may oppoſe, but which the ſins
" and ſwords of tyrants cannot deſtroy.
" We lay claim to no ſort of ſuperiority
" over you. We aſpire but at the honour
" of equality. This glory is ſufficient for
" us. We know too well the ineſtimable
" value of governing ourſelves, to wiſh
" henceforward that you ſhould be diveſted
" of the boon.

    " If, ſupreme maſters and arbiters of
" your legiſlation, you can create for your
" ſtates a better government than ours, we
" give you anticipated joy. Your happi-
" neſs will inſpire us with no other ſenti-
" ment, than the deſire of imitation.

F

                                 " Form

" Form for yourſelves conſtitutions adapt-
" ed to your climate, to your ſoil, to this
" new world you civiliſe. Who better
" than yourſelves can know your peculiar
" wants? High-ſpirited and virtuous minds,
" like yours, ſhould obey but the laws
" which ſhall be given them by themſelves.
" All other reſtraint would be unworthy
" of them. Regulate your own taxation.
" We deſire you only to conform your-
" ſelves to our cuſtom in the aſſeſſment of
" the duties. We will preſent to you a
" ſtate of our wants; and you will of your-
" ſelves aſſign the juſt proportion between
" your ſuccours and your riches.

" Moreover, exerciſe your induſtry, like
" us ; without limitation exerciſe it. A-
" vail yourſelves of the benefits of nature,
" and of the fruitful countries you inha-
" bit. Let the iron of your mines, the
" wool of your flocks, the ſkins of the ſa-
" vage animals which wander in your
" woods, faſhioned in your manufactures,
" take a new value from your hands. Be
" your ports free. Go, and expoſe to
" ſale the productions of your lands, and
" of

" of your arts, in all the quarters of the
" world. Go, and feek for thofe of which
" you ftand in need. It is one of our pri-
" vileges, let it be likewife yours. The
" empire of the ocean, which we have ac-
" quired by two ages of greatnefs and
" glory, belongs as well to you as us.
" We fhall be united by the ties of com-
" merce. You will bring us your pro-
" ductions, which we fhall receive in pre-
" ference to thofe of all other people, and
" we hope that you will prefer ours to
" thofe of foreigners, without being re-
" ftrained to it however by any law, but
" that of the common intereft, and the
" fair claims of countrymen and friends.

    " Let the fhips of your country and of
" ours, adorned by the fame ftreamer,
" overfpread the feas; and let fhouts of
" joy arife on each fide, when fifter-veffels
" meet each other in the deferts of the
" ocean. Let peace fpring up again be-
" tween us, and concord laft for ever.
" We are fenfible at length, that the chain
" of mutual benevolence is the only one,
" which can bind fuch diftant empires to-

" gether,

" gether, and that every other principle
" of unity would be precarious and unjuft.
" Upon this new plan of eternal amity,
" let agriculture, induftry, laws, arts, and
" the firft of all fciences, that of procur-
" ing the greateft good to communities
" and individuals, be perfected amongft
" you. Let the recital of your happinefs
" call around you all the unfortunate of
" the earth. Let the tyrants of all coun-
" tries, let all oppreffors, political or fa-
" cred, know, that there exifts upon the
" earth a place, where a deliverance from
" their chains is to be found ; where af-
" flicted, dejected humanity has lifted up
" her head ; where harvefts grow for the
" poor; where laws are no more than
" the fecurity of happinefs; where reli-
" gion is free, and confcience has ceafed
" to be a flave; where, in fhort, nature
" feems to put in her plea of juftification,
" for having created man ; and govern-
" ment, fo long time guilty, over all the
" earth, makes at laft the reparation of
" its crimes. Let the idea of fuch an
" afylum ferve as a terror and reftraint
" to

" to defpots : for if they have no kindnefs
" about their hearts, and look with indiffe-
" rence on the happinefs of man, they have
" at leaft much avarice and ambition, which
" muft make them anxious to preferve
" both their riches and their power.

" We ourfelves, O countrymen, O
" friends, we ourfelves fhall profit by your
" example. If our conftitution fhould be
" altered for the worfe ; if public riches
" fhould corrupt the court, and the court
" the nation ; if our kings, to whom we
" have given fo many terrible examples,
" fhould at laft forget them ; if we fhould
" be in danger, we who were an auguft
" people, of dwindling to a vile herd of
" abjects, by bafely fetting ourfelves to
" fale ; we might be re-animated by the
" fight of your virtues and your laws.
" It might recall to our depraved and
" daftard hearts, with a fenfe of the value
" and the grandeur of liberty, the energy
" to preferve it. But if it muft be, that
" fuch an example as yours fhall want
" power to prompt us ; if it muft be, that
" flavery, the never-failing follower of ve-

" nality,

" nality, fhall be, one day, eftablifhed in
" that land, which has been inundated
" with blood in the caufe of freedom,
" which has feen fcaffolds erected for the
" punifhment of tyrants; then will we
" emigrate like your fathers, then will we
" abandon, in a body, the ungrateful ifle,
" delivered up to a defpot, and leave the
" monfter, to reign and roar, in a defert
" for domain.   Then fhall you furely wel.
" come us as friends, as brothers.   You
" will fuffer us to partake with you of this
" foil, of this air, free as the generous
" fouls of their inhabitants, and, thanks
" to your virtues, we fhall find again an
" England, again a country.

   " Such, brave countrymen, are our
" hopes, fuch our wifhes.   Receive then
" our oaths, pledges of fo holy an alliance.
" Let us invoke, to ftill add folemnity
" to the treaty, let us invoke our common
" anceftors, who were all animated by
" the fpirit of liberty like you, and did
" not dread to die in its defence.   Let
" us call to witnefs, the memory of the
" illuftrious founders of your colonies,

6   " that

" that of your auguſt legiſlators, of the
" philoſophic Locke, the firſt man upon
" the earth who made a code of tole-
" ration, of the venerable Penn, the firſt
" who founded a city of brethren. The
" ſpirits of theſe great men, who ſurely at
" this moment are beholding us with
" earneſtneſs and with pleaſure, are wor-
" thy to preſide at a treaty, which is about
" to draw the bleſſings of peace upon a
" double-world. Swear we, in their pre-
" ſence; ſwear we, upon the very arms,
" with which you have ſo valiantly with-
" ſtood us; ſwear we, to remain for ever
" united, and for ever true; and when the
" oath of peace ſhall have been pro-
" nounced by all, make, of theſe ſame
" arms, a ſacred depoſite in ſome hallowed
" pile, where the fathers ſhall ſhew them
" to the generations as they riſe; and
" there keep them carefully from age to
" age, in order to their being, one day,
" turned againſt the firſt, be he Engliſh or
" American, who ſhall dare propoſe the
" rupture of that alliance, which is equally
F 4
" uſeful,

" ufeful, equally honourable to both the
" names."

At this difcourfe, I hear the towns, the
villages, the fields, all the fhores of North
America refound, with livelieft acclama-
tion, with tendereft repetition of the en-
dearing names of brother and of mother,
applied to your country and her fons. And
whilft the conflagrations of war are fucceeded by bonfires and fports, and every
demonftration of a heart felt triumphant
joy, I fee the nations, envious of your
power, to ftand aghaft, in filence, aftonifh-
ment, defpair.

Your parliament is about to meet. What
is to be expected from it ? Will it liften
to reafon, or will it perfevere in its madnefs ? Will it be the defender of the
rights of nations, or the inftrument of the
tyranny of minifters ? Will its acts be the
decrees of a free people, or edicts dictated
by the court ? I am prefent at the deliberations of your houfes. In thefe revered
reforts I hear wifdom fpeak by the mouth
of moderation. Soft perfuafion feems to
flow there, from the lips of moft diftin-
guifhed

guifhed orators. My heart is filled with
hope : my eyes over run with tears. Prefently a voice, the organ of defpotifm and
of war, fufpends the delicious, fweet emo-
tion.

" Englifhmen, cries a mad haranguer,
" can you hefitate a moment ? It is your
" rights, it is your moft important inte-
" refts, it is the glory of your name, that
" you are called upon to defend. It is
" not a foreign power which attacks thefe
" effential objects. They are menaced by
" an interior, domeftic enemy. The dan-
" ger therefore is more imminent, the
" outrage the more fenfible.

" Between two rival powers, armed for
" mutual pretenfions, policy may fome-
" times fufpend hoftilities. Againft rebel
" fubjects, flacknefs is the greateft fault,
" and all moderation weaknefs. The
" ftandard of revolt, which was fet up by
" audacity, fhould be torn down by power.
" Let the fword of juftice fall heavy on
" the hands which dared difplay it. Let
" us be expeditious. In thefe cafes there
" is a firft moment which muft be feized
" on ;

" on ; revolutions fhould be ftrangled in
" their birth. Give not to minds, yet in
" amazement, time to grow familiar with
" their guilt; to the ringleaders, time to
" confirm their power; nor to the peo-
" ple, that of learning to obey new maf-
" ters. The people, in a revolt, are al-
" moft always actuated by alien impulfes.
" Neither their fury, nor their hatred,
" nor their love, are properly their own.
" You may give them paffions, as eafily as
" arms. Difplay to their eyes, the power
" and majefty of the Britifh empire : they
" will prefently be falling at your feet ;
" and go in an inftant from terror to
" compunction, from compunction to obe-
" dience. If we muft have recourfe to
" the feverity of arms, let us have
" no fcruples. In civil war, pity is a
" moft miftaken virtue. When the fword
" is once drawn, it ought not to be ftayed,
" but by fubmiffion. It is for them to
" anfwer now, to heaven and to earth,
" for the evils which they bring upon
" themfelves. Confider that a tranfient
" feverity, in thefe rebellious countries,
" will

" will infure us peace and obedience that
" will laft for ages.

" In order to make us fufpend our
" blows, and difarm our hands, we have
" heen told, and told repeatedly, that the
" land is peopled by our countrymen, by
" our friends, by our brethren. What,
" invoke in their favour names which they
" have outraged, bands which they have
" broken? Thefe names, thefe bands, fo
" facred, are the very thing that accufes
" and attaints them. Since when, were
" thefe revered titles to impofe duties but
" on us? Since when, had rebellious
" children the right to take arms againft
" their mother, defpoil her of her heri-
" tage, and rend her heart? They talk
" of liberty : I refpect this name as much
" as they do ; but by this liberty, is it
" independance, that we are to under-
" ftand? · Is it the right, to overturn a
" legiflation, founded and eftablifhed two
" ages fince? Is it the right, to ufurp
" all thofe which we poffefs? They talk
" of liberty, but I talk, and will always
                                    " talk,

" talk, of the fupremacy, and the fove-
" reign power, of Britain.

" What, fuppofing they had fome caufes
" of complaint, fuppofing they intended
" to refufe bearing fome light portion of
" the heavy burden under which we ftag-
" ger, to refufe unreafonably to make
" themfelves partners in our expences, as
" we have made them partners in our
" greatnefs, had they no other way to do
" it, than by revolt and arms? There are
" thofe who call them our countrymen,
" and our friends; but, for my part, I
" can fee them in no other light than
" that of the moft cruel perfecutors and
" enemies of our country. We had com-
" mon fathers, it is faid; and fo, undoubt-
" edly, we had: but thefe refpectable an-
" ceftors I myfelf with confidence invoke.
" If their fpirits could here refume their
" places, their indignation would not be
" inferior to our own. With what wrath
" would thefe virtuous citizens then un-
" derftand, that thofe of their children
" who went to fix themfelves beyond the
" feas, no fooner began to be a little

4   " confcious

" confcious of their ftrength, than they
" made a traitorous trial of it againft
" their country; armed themfelves againft
" her with the very benefits her bounty
" had beftowed ? Yes, all; even to that
" pacific fect, enjoined ftrictly by their
" founder never to dip their hands in
" blood; they, who have refpected the
" lives and the rights of favage people;
" they, who by an enthufiafm of huma-
" nity, have ftruck off the fetters from
" their flaves : now, equally faithlefs to
" their country and their religion, they
" arm their hands for flaughter ; and it is
" againft you. They treat all men as bre-
" thren; and you, you only, of all peo-
" ple, are excluded from the title. They
" have fhewn the world that the favages
" of America, that the negroes of Africa,
" are henceforward lefs alien to them than
" the citizens of Britain.

" Arm, then, arm. Britons, ftrike
" home ; revenge, revenge, your coun-
" try's wrongs, your offended rights. Re-
" venge the treafon to your greatnefs. Dif-
" play that power, fo redoutable in Eu-
" rope,

" rope, in Africa, and the Indies; which
" has fo often aftonifhed America herfelf;
" and fince between a fovereign-people
" and the fubject-people who revolt, there
" can be no treaty now, but force, let
" force decide. Snatch opportunely at
" this world, which is falling from you,
" and refume it; it is your property,
" which ingratitude and infolence would
" ravifh from you."

England
determines
to reduce
her colonies
by force.

The fophifms of a fretting, ftrutting
fpeechifier, upheld by royal power and national pride, fupprefs, in the majority of
the reprefentatives of the people, the defire of pacific meafures. New refolutions
refemble thofe which begot them; but
with aggravated features of ferocity and
defpotifm. Levies of troops, equipments
of fleets. Admirals and generals fet fail
for the new world, with orders and projects
fanguinary and favage. Nothing lefs than
unconditional fubmiffion can reftrain or
retard the devaftation ordained againft the
colonies.

Until this memorable period, the Americans had confined themfelves to a refiftance,

ance, authorized even by the Englifh laws.
No other ambition appeared in them, than
that of maintaining the very limited rights
which they had hitherto enjoyed. Even
the leading men amongft them, who might
be fuppofed to have more enlarged ideas,
had not yet ventured to fpeak to the multitude of any thing but an advantageous
accommodation. They would have been
afraid, in going further, of lofing the confidence of people attached by habit to an
empire, under whofe wings they had prof-
pered. The accounts of the great preparations which were making in the old world,
with fetters to confine, or with fire to con-
fume, the new, extinguifhed all remains
of affection for the original government.
The only bufinefs now, was to give energy
to minds ready to receive it. This was
the effect which a work, intituled " *Com-*
" *mon Senfe,*" produced. We fhall give
here the fum and fubftance of its doctrine,
without tying ourfelves down to its exact
form and order.

Never, fays the author of this celebrated
performance, never did a more grand con-
cernment

cernment call for the attention of the world.
It is not that of a city or a province, it is
that of an immenfe continent, and of a
confiderable portion of the globe. It is
not the affair of a day, it is that of ages.
The prefent is about to decide upon a long
futurity; and many hundreds of years after
that we fhall be no more, the fun, in illu-
minating this hemifphere, will illuminate
our glory, or expofe our fhame. A long
time did we fpeak of peace and reconcile-
ment : all is changed. On the day when,
in confequence of the recourfe which has
been had to arms, the firft drop of blood
was fhed, time for difquifition paffed away.
A day has given birth to a revolution. A
day has tranfported us to another age.

Timid fouls, fouls who meafure the future by the paft, think that we ftand in
need of the protection of England. That
protection might be ufeful to a rifing colony ; it is become dangerous for a nation
formed. Infancy muft needs be fupported,
in its weak endeavours to walk ; youth
fhould march actively and freely, in power
and pride of port. The nation, as well as
the

the man, who may have the power and
right to protect me, may have the power
and will to opprefs me. I give up the fupport of a protector, to be fecured from the
fear of a mafter.

In Europe, the people are too much
agitated to allow to this part of the world
the enjoyment of conftant peace. In thofe
courts and nations interefts meet interefts,
and joftle without end. As friends of England we muft neceffarily have all her enemies for our own. This alliance will en-
tail upon America the dower of perpetual
war. Let us part, let us part. Neutra-
lity, trade and peace; fuch, and fuch only,
can be the foundations of our greatnefs.

The authority of Great Britain over
America muft fooner or later be extinct.
So wills nature, neceffity, and time. The
Englifh government can, therefore, give
us only a tranfient conftitution; and we
fhall bequeath to our pofterity but debts,
and diffenfions, and a precarious ftate.
If we would infure their happinefs, let us
part. If we are fathers, if we love our

G   children,

children, let us part. Laws and liberty
are the heritage we owe them.

England is too far removed from us ; we
cannot be governed by fuch a diftant country. What, to traverfe, always, two thoufand leagues, to claim juftice, or to afk
for laws ! to exculpate ourfelves from imaginary crimes, or folicit, with meannefs,
the court and minifters of a foreign clime !
What, to wait for years for every anfwer ;
and to find, as we might too often, when
we had croffed and recroffed the ocean, that
injuftice only would be the product of our
voyage ! No ; to be a great ftate, the centre and the feat of power muft be in the
ftate itfelf. Nothing but the defpotifm of
the Eaft can inure men thus to receive their
laws from rulers far remote, or from the
bafhaws, by whom invifible tyrants are re-
prefented. But let it not be forgotten, that
the more the diftance is augmented, the
more ponderous and cruel is the preffure of
the defpotic power ; and the people then,
deprived of almoft all the advantages of
government, feel only its miferies and its
vices.

Nature

Nature did not create a world to fubject it to the inhabitants of an ifland. Nature has eftablifhed the laws of equilibrium, which fhe every where obferves, in the heavens as well as upon the earth. By the laws of bodies, and of diftances, America can belong but to itfelf.

There is no government without a mutual confidence between him who commands and him who obeys. It is all over; this mutual confidence is gone, and never can return. England has too clearly fhewn that fhe would command us like flaves; America, that fhe was equally fenfible both of her rights and of her ftrength. They have each betrayed their fecret. From this moment there can be no further treaty. It would be figned by hatred and diftruft; hatred, which never pardons; diftruft, which, by its very nature, can never be reconciled.

Would you know what an accommodation would produce? Your ruin. You ftand in need of laws; you will not obtain them. Who would give them to you? The Englifh nation? She is jealous of your

increafe. The   ? He is your enemy.
Yourfelves, in your affemblies? Do you
not remember that all legiflation is fub-
mitted to the negative right of the monarch who would bring you to his yoke >
This right would be a formidable right
inceffantly armed againft you. Make re-
quefts; they will be eluded. Form pleas
of commerce and greatnefs; they will become to the mother-country an object of
affright. Your government will be no
more than a kind of clandeftine war; that
of an enemy who would deftroy without
openly attacking; it will be, according to
the ordinary courfe of policy, a flow and
fecret affaffination, which will caufe lan-
gour and prolong weaknefs, and, with the
art of an imperial torturer, equally prohibit you to live or die. Submit to England; and behold your fate.

It is not without right that we take
arms. Our right is neceffity, a juft defence, the miferies of ourfelves and of our
children, the exceffes committed againft
us. Our right is our auguft title of nation. It is for the fword to judge us
                                    The

The tribunal of war, is the only tribunal which now exiſts for us. Well then, ſince the ſword muſt neceſſarily be drawn, let us be ſure at leaſt, that it be for a cauſe that may be worthy of it, and requite us for both our treaſure and our blood. What, ſhall we expoſe ourſelves to the ſeeing our habitations ruined, our lands laid waſte, our families ſlaughtered, in order to com-paſs at laſt an accommodation; that is, to implore new chains, and cement our-ſelves the edifice of our bondage? What, ſhall it be by the dreadful light of confla-grations, ſhall it be on the tomb of our fathers, or our children, or our wives, that we ſhall ſign a treaty with our proud op-preſſors! and, all covered with our blood, will they deign to pardon us! Ah, we ſhould then be but a vile object of pitying wonder to Europe, of indignation to Ame-rica, and of contempt even to our enemies. If we can obey them, we had not the right to combat them. Liberty only can ab-ſolve us. Liberty, and perfect liberty, is the only object worthy of our labours and our dangers. What do I ſay? From this

moment

moment it is our own. Our title is written on the bloody plains of Lexington; it was there that the hand of England tore the contract by which we were united to her. Yes. At the moment when the report of the firft mufquet difcharged by England was heard, nature herfelf proclaimed us free and independent.

Let us profit by the benefit of foes. The youth of nations is the age moft favourable to their independence. It is the time of energy and vigour. Our fouls are not yet furrounded by that apparatus of luxury, which ferves as hoftage to a tyrant. Our arms are not yet enervated in the arts of foftnefs. Amongft us are not feen to domineer thofe nobles, who, by their very conftitution, are the neceffary allies of kings; who love not liberty, but when they can make of it an inftrument of op preffion; thofe nobles, eager for privilege and title, for whom, in critical conjunc tures, the people are but tools, for whom the fupreme power is a ready corruptor.

Your colonies are formed of plain, brave, laborious, upright men, proprietors and cultivators

cultivators of their land in one. Liberty
is their firſt want. Rural labours have already hardened them for war. Public enthuſiaſm brings to light unknown talents.
It is in revolutions that great minds are
formed, that heroes ſhew themſelves, and
take their place. Remember Holland, and
all her ſons; and that number of extraordinary men to which the quarrel of her liberty gave birth : behold in theſe men an
example for you ; remember their ſuccefs
and behold a preſage.

Let our firſt ſtep be to form a conſtitu-
tion by which we may be united. The
moment is arrived. Later, it would be
abandoned to an uncertain futurity and the
caprice of chance. The more people and
riches we ſhall acquire, the more barriers
will there be raiſed up between us. Then,
how ſhall ſo many provinces and intereſts
be made conſiſtent ? For ſuch an union,
it is neceſſary that each people ſhould at
once be ſenſible, both of the particular
weakneſs, and the general ſtrength. There
muſt be great calamities or great fears. It
is then, amongſt communities as amongſt
G 4 individuals,

individuals, that fpring up thofe firm and vigorous friendfhips which affociate fouls with fouls, and interefts with interefts. It is then, that one fpirit, breathed from every part, forms the genius of ftates; and that all the fcattered powers become by union a fingle and a formidable power. Thanks to our perfecutors, we are at this epocha. If we have courage, it will be that of our happinefs. Few nations have laid hold of the favourable moment to form their government. Once efcaped, this moment returns no more; and anarchy or flavery punifhes the neglect of it for ages. Let not a fimilar fault prepare for us fimilar regret. Regret is impotent.

Let the moment, which, in refpect to us, is fingular, be feized on. We have it in our power to frame the fineft conftitution that the world has feen. You have read in your facred books how mankind were deftroyed by the general deluge. A fingle family furvived, and was commanded by the Supreme Being to re-people the earth. We are this family. Defpotifm

has

has deluged all; and we can a fecond time renew the world.

We are about, at this moment, to decide the fate of a race of men more numerous perhaps than all the people of Europe put together. Shall we wait till we may be the prey of a conqueror, and fuffer the hope of the univerfe to be deftroyed? Imagine to yourfelves, that all the generations of the world to come, have at this moment their eyes fixed on us, and demand of us their liberty. We are about to fix their deftiny. If we give them up, they will, perhaps, one day, drag their chains acrofs our tombs, and load them with imprecations.

Call to mind a writing which has appeared amongft you, and had for a motto, UNITE OR DIE.

Let us unite then, and began by declaring our INDEPENDENCE. That alone can efface the name of rebellious fubjects, which our infolent oppreffors have dared to give us. That alone can make us rife up to the dignity which is our due, infure us allies amongft the powers, imprefs refpect even

upon

upon our enemies, and, if we treat with them, give us the right to treat, with the power and majesty which becomes a nation.

But I repeat it; we must be quick. Our uncertainty makes our weakness. Let us dare to be free, and we are so. Ready to take the leap, we draw back. We read the countenances of each other with anxious curiosity. It seems, as if we were astonished at our own boldness, and that our very courage gave us fear. But it is not now the time to be musing on calculations. It is passed. In great affairs, in which there is but one great part to take, too much circumspection ceases to be prudence. Every thing that is extreme, demands resolution in the extreme. Then, the boldest measures are the wisest; and the excess of boldness itself becomes the means and the warrant of success.

The colonies break the ties which united them to England, and declare themselves independent of her.

Such was the substance of the sentiments displayed in this work. They confirmed in their principles the enterprizing spirits who had long required a total separation from the mother-country. The timid citizens, who had been wavering till then, now

3

now declared decifively for this great and interefting rupture. The votaries of inde-pendance were numerous enough to bring the general congrefs, on the 4th of July, 1776, to the determination to pronounce it.

Why have I not received the genius and the eloquence of the celebrated orators of Athens and of Rome! With what gran-deur, with what enthufiafm, fhould I not fpeak of thofe generous men who erected this grand edifice, by their patience, their wifdom, and their courage! Hancock, Franklin, the two Adamfes, were the great-eft actors in this affecting fcene : but they were not the only ones. Pofterity fhall know them all. Their honoured names fhall be tranfmitted to it by a happier pen than mine. Brafs and marble fhall fhew them to remoteft ages. In beholding them, fhall the friend of freedom feel his heart palpitate with joy, feel his eyes floating in delicious tears. Under the buft of one of them has been written; HE WRESTED THUNDER FROM HEAVEN AND THE SCEPTRE

FROM

FROM TYRANTS *. Of the laſt words of
this eulogy ſhall all of them partake.

Heroic country, my advanced age permits me not to viſit thee. Never ſhall I
ſee myſelf amongſt the reſpectable perſon-
ages of thy Areopagus; never ſhall I be
preſent at the deliberations of thy congreſs.
I ſhall die without having ſeen the retreat
of toleration, of manners, of laws, of virtue, and of freedom. My aſhes will not
be covered by a free and holy earth : but I
ſhall have deſired it; and my laſt breath
ſhall bear to heaven an ejaculation for thy
proſperity.

Though America might be aſſured of
univerſal approbation, ſhe thought it in-
cumbent on her to expoſe to the eyes of
the world the motives of her conduct.
She publiſhed her manifeſto, in which we
read that,

" The hiſtory of the Engliſh nation and
" its king will ſhew to the ſucceeding ge-
" nerations, whom it ſhall entertain and in

* *Eripuit cœlo fulmen, ſceptrumque tyrannis,* is
the line applied to the great Electrician : and the
tranſlator dares not criticiſe a line which his maſter
has thought worthy to be ſtudded in his work.

I   " ſtruct

" ſtruck with accounts of them and us, a
" ſeries of outrages and of uſurpations,
" which vied with each other in their
" tendency to eſtabliſh abſolute tyranny
" in theſe provinces.

" It will ſhew, that the monarch refuſed
" his conſent to laws the moſt ſalutary and
" the moſt neceſſary to the public good.

" That he removed the aſſemblies to
" inconvenient places, at a diſtance from
" all records, in order to bring the depu-
" ties more eaſily to his views.

" That he had frequently diſſolved the
" aſſembly of repreſentatives, becauſe they
" had firmly defended the people's rights.

" That, after ſuch diſſolution, he had left
" the ſtates too long without repreſenta-
" tives, and conſequently expoſed to the
" inconveniences reſulting from the want
" of aſſemblies.

" That he endeavoured to hinder po-
" pulation, by raiſing difficulties to the
" naturalization of foreigners, and by ſell-
" ing the lands, of which he granted the
" property, too dear.

" That he made the judges too depen-
" dant on himſelf, by decreeing that they
" ſhould

" fhould hold but of him alone, both
" their offices and their falaries.

" That he created new employments
" and filled this country with a multitude
" of place-men, who devoured our fub-
" ftance and difturbed our quiet.

" That he maintained amongft us, in
" time of profound peace, a confiderable
" number of troops, without the confent
" of the legiflative power.

" That he rendered military power in-
" dependent of, and even fuperior to, the
" civil power.

" That he contrived all means, in con-
" junction with perverfe men, to quarter
" armed foldiers in our houfes, and exempt
" them from the pains due to the murders
" they might commit in America; to de-
" ftroy our trade in all parts of the world;
" to impofe taxes on us without our con-
" fent; to deprive us, in many cafes, of
" our trials by juries; to tranfport us,
" and make us take our trials, beyond
" the feas; to take away our charters,
" fupprefs our beft laws, to alter the
" foundation and the form of our govern-
" ment

" ment for the worfe; to fufpend our
" own legiflation, and make us receive
" other laws.

" That he himfelf abdicated his go-
" vernment in the American provinces,
" by declaring us fallen from his protec-
" tion, and by making war upon us.

" That he caufed our coafts to be ra-
" vaged, our ports to be deftroyed, our
" towns to be burnt, our people to be
" maffacred.

" That he forced thofe who were taken
" prifoners upon the high feas, to bear
" arms againft their country, to become
" the executioners of their friends and bre-
" thren, or to perifh themfelves by hands
" fo dear.

" That he excited amongft us inteftine
" divifions; and that he endeavoured to
" raife againft our peaceable inhabitants,
" the barbarous favages, accuftomed to
" maffacre all, without diftinction of rank,
" fex, and age.

" That at this time there arrived on
" our fhores foreign mercenaries, com-
" miffioned

" miffioned to compleat the work of de-
" vaftation and death.

" And that a prince, whofe character
" was thus marked by all the features of
" tyranny, was not fit to govern a free
" people."

A ftep which broke the ties formed by
blood, by religion, and by habit, was to be
fupported by a grand concert of wills, by
wife and vigorous meafures. The United
States of America gave themfelves a federate conftitution, which joined, to the interior advantages of republican government,
all the power of monarchy.

Each province had an affembly formed
by the reprefentatives of the different diftricts, and in which the legiflative power
refided. The executive power was committed to its prefident. His rights and
his obligations were, to liften to every ap-
plication from any of the people; to call
them together when circumftances might
require it; to provide for the arming and
fubfifting troops, and concert the operations
of them with their officers. He was at the
head of a fecret committee, which was to
hold

hold a continual correfpondence with the general congrefs. The time of his conti-nuance in office was limited to two years But the laws permitted a prolongation of it.

The provinces were not obliged to ren-der an account of their adminiftration to the great council of the nation, though compofed of the deputies of all the colo-nies. The fuperiority of the general con-grefs over the particular congreffes was confined to matters relative to politics and war.

But fome people have thought that the inftitution of this body was not fo well contrived as the legiflation of the provinces. It feems, it muft be confeffed, that federate ftates, which raife themfelves from the con-dition of fubjects up to that of being inde-pendent, cannot without danger truft their delegates with the unlimited power of making peace and war. For thefe dele-gates, fhould they be corrupt or ill in-formed, might bring back the whole ftate to the bondage which it is feeking to efcape from. It feems, that in thefe times of re-

H   volution,

volution, the public will cannot be too
well known, too literally pronounced. It
is neceffary, undoubtedly, they fay, that
all the meafures, all the operations, which
relate to the common defence and offence,
fhould be decided on by the common reprefentatives of the body of the ftate: but
the continuation of war, and the conditions
of peace, ought to be deliberated upon in
every province; and the deliberations to
be tranfmitted to the congrefs by the deputies, who would fubmit the opinion of their
provinces to the plurality of voices. In
fhort, they add, that if in eftablifhed governments it is proper that the people
fhould rely with confidence in the wifdom
of their fenate, in a ftate where the conftitution is forming, where the people, as yet
uncertain of their fate, call for their liberty,
fword in hand, it is neceffary that all the
citizens fhould be continually in council,
in camp, in the public places, and have
their eyes continually open upon the reprefentatives to whom their deftiny has been
committed.

2   Though

Though thefe principles are true in general, there might be a difficulty, we may
anfwer, in applying them to the new republic formed by the Americans. It is
not with that republic as with the federate
republics which we fee in Europe, I mean
Holland and Switzerland, which occupy a
country but of fmall extent, and in which
it is eafy to eftablifh a rapid communication between all the provinces. The fame
thing may be faid of the confederacies of
ancient Greece. Thefe ftates were fituated
at a fmall diftance from each other, confined almoft within the narrow compafs of
the Peloponnefus, or, at moft, within the
limits of the Achipelago. But the United
States of America, difperfed over an immenfe continent; occupying in the new
world a fpace of almoft fifteen degrees;
feparated by deferts, by mountains, by
gulfs, and by a vaft extent of coaft, cannot
have the advantage of this rapid communication. If the general congrefs could
not decide upon political interefts without
the particular deliberations of each province; if on every important occafion, on

H 2 every

every unforeseen event, it should be necessary to give new inſtructions, and, as we
may ſay, a new power to the repreſentatives, this body would remain inactive.
The diſtances to be paſſed, the delays and
the multitude of debates, might too often
be hurtful to the public good.

Beſides, it is never at the birth of a con-
ſtitution, and amidſt the great fermenta-
tions of liberty, that there is cauſe to fear
that a body of repreſentatives ſhould, either
from weakneſs or corruption, betray the
intereſts with which they are entruſted. It
is rather in ſuch a body that the general
ſpirit is both exalted and inflamed. In
that reſides, in its vigour, the genius of the
nation. Choſen by the eſteem of their
fellow-citizens, choſen at a time when every
public function is a danger, and every vote
an honour, placed at the head of thoſe who
will compoſe for ever that celebrated areopagus, and thence even naturally carried
to regard the public liberty as their own
work, they cannot but have the enthuſiaſm
of founders, who make it their pride to
have their names engraved conſpicuouſly,

to

to be read by diftant ages, on the frontif-
piece of an auguft monument which is
rifing. The fears which the partifans of
the contrary fyftem might have upon this
object, feem therefore to have fmall foundation.

I will fay more. It might happen that
a people who are fighting for liberty, fatigued with a long and painful ftruggle,
and more ftruck with the prefent danger
than the future good, might feel their courage failing, and perhaps, one day, be
tempted to prefer dependence and peace to
independence and tumult, attended with
peril and with blood. Then would it be
advantageous to this people to have di-
vefted themfelves of the power of making
peace with their oppreffors, and depofited
it in the hands of the fenate which they
had chofen to ferve as an organ to their
will, when this will could fhew itfelf with
freedom, pride, and courage. It feems as
if each individual, when he had given his
voice for the inftituting fuch a fenate,
fhould fay to it, I raife the ftandard of
war againft my tyrants. If my arm fhould

weary

weary in the war, if I could debafe myfelf
fo low as to implore repofe, fupport me
againft my weaknefs.   Liften to no prayer
or wifh unworthy of me, which I difavow
beforehand ; and pronounce not the name
of peace until my bonds be broken.

In reality, if we confult the hiftory of
republics, we fhall fee, that the multitude
have almoft always great impetuofity and
heat at the firft moment ; but that it is
only in a fmall number of chofen men,
and qualified to ferve as chiefs, that re-
fide thofe conftant and vigorous refolutions
which march, with a fteady, firm, undaunt-
ed ftep, towards fome great and worthy
end, never turning, or looking, from the
path, and never ceafing, moft ftubbornly
to combat all obftructions that they meet
with, from fortune, from mifery, and from
man.

Commence-
ment of the
war between
the United
States and
England.
However it be, and whatfoever fide may
be taken in this political difcuffion, the
Americans had not yet created for themfelves a fyftem of government, when in
the month of March, Hopkins plundered
the Ifland of Providence of a large train
of

of artillery and a confiderable quantity of ammunition; when in the beginning of May, Carleton drove out of Canada the Provincial troops, which were employed to reduce Quebec with a view of completing the conqueft of that important territory; when in the month of June Clinton and Parker had been fo vigoroufly repulfed on the Southern coafts of America. Far greater fcenes followed the declaration of independence.

Howe had been appointed to fuperfede the feeble Gage: and it was this new general who had evacuated Bofton. Having arrived on the 2d of April at Halifax, on the 10th of June he departed for Staten Ifland. The forces, which were to act both by fea and land, fucceffively joined him according to expectation; and on the 28th of Auguft he landed on Long-Ifland without oppofition, under the protection of a Fleet commanded by the admiral his brother. The Americans exhibited as little fpirit in defending the interior part of their country as they did on the landing of the enemy.

After

After a very feeble refiftance, and confiderable lofs, they took refuge on the continent with a facility, which would hardly
have been granted them by a conqueror,
who knew how to avail himfelf of the advantages he had obtained. The city of
New-York too was abandoned by thefe
new republicans with ftill greater precipitation than they had evacuated Long-
Ifland : and they filed off towards Kingf-
bridge, where they appeared determined
to make an obftinate refiftance.

If the Englifh had followed up their
fuccefs with that vivacity which circumftances demanded, the new-raifed troops
which had oppofed them had infallibly
been difperfed, or reduced to the neceffity
of laying down their arms. On the contrary, they were allowed fix weeks to recover from their confternation : nor did they
abandon their intrenchments till the night
of the firft or fecond of November, when
the movements, which were making in
their view, were fufficient to convince them
that their camp was upon the point of being attacked.

Their

Their commander in chief, Wafhington, was unwilling to truft the fate of his country to an action, which might and naturally would have terminated to the prejudice of thofe important interefts which had been committed to him. He knew, that delays, ever favourable to a native, arc ever fatal to a ftranger. This conviction determined him to retire to the Jerfeys with a defign of protracting the war. Favoured both by the inclemency of the feafon, by his knowledge of the country, and by the nature of the ground, which compenfated in fome meafure for the want of difcipline, he had reafon to flatter himfelf, that he fhould be able to cover the greateft part of this fertile province, and keep the enemy at a diftance from Penfylvania. In a moment, however, he fees his colours abandoned by the foldiers, whofe engagement, at the end of fix, and even at the end of three months, had expired : and of an army of twenty five thoufand men, there fcarce remained two thoufand five hundred, with which he was fortunate enough to retire beyond the Delawar.

Without

Without lofing a moment, the King's troops ought to have paffed the river in purfuit of this handful of fugitives, and have put them totally to the rout. If the five thoufand men, deftined for the conqueft of Rhode-Ifland, had gone up the river in the tranfports they were aboard of, the junction of the two corps might have been effected without oppofition even in Philadelphia itfelf, and the new republic had been ftifled in that important and celebrated city which gave it birth.

At this time, perhaps, reproaches were caft on the Englifh general for being timid and too circumfpect in the operations of the campaign. Certain it is, however, that he was rafh enough in the diftribution of his winter-cantonments. They were difpofed in fuch a manner, as if there remained not in America a fingle individual, who had either inclination or power to moleft them.

This prefumption encouraged the militia of Pennfylvania, Maryland and Virginia, collected together and reunited for the fupport of the common caufe.

On

On the 25th of December they croffed
the Delaware, and fell accidentally upon
Trenton, which was occupied by fifteen
hundred of the twelve thoufand Heffians,
fold in fo bafe a manner, by their avaricious
mafter, to the King of Great Britain. This
corps was maffacred, taken, or entirely difperfed. Eight days after three Englifh re-
giments were in like manner driven from
Prince-town, but after having better fupported their reputation than the foreign
troops in their pay.

Thefe unexpected events reduced the
enemies of America, in the Jerfeys, to the
neceffity of confining their pofts to Amboy
and Brunfwick, where yet they were ex-
ceedingly harraffed during the remainder
of the winter.

The effect of ftrong paffions, and of
great dangers, is often to aftonifh the mind,
and to throw it into that kind of torpor
that deprives it of the ufe of its powers;
by degrees it recovers and collects itfelf:
all its faculties, fufpended for a moment,
difplay themfelves with redoubled vigour:
every fpring of action is awakened, and it
feels

feels its powers rife at once to a level with the difficulties it has to encounter. In a great multitude there are always fome who feel this immediate effect, which rapidly communicates itfelf to others. Such a revolution took place amongft the confederate ftates. It caufed armed men to iffue from all quarters.

It was very late before the campaign of 1777 was opened. The Englifh army, in defpair of penetrating into Penfylvania by way of the Jerfeys, at laft embarked on the 23d of July, and, by the bay of Chefapeak, landed in a country which their generals may very juftly be reproached for not having invaded the year before. Their march is uninterrupted, till they reach Brandywine. There, on the 11th of September, they attack and beat the Americans, and arrive on the 30th at Philadelphia, which had been abandoned on the 25th by the Congrefs, and a few days later or fooner by the greateft number of the inhabitants.

This victory is attended with no confequences. The conqueror fees nothing
around

around him but hatred and devaſtation.
Pent up in a ſpace extremely circumſcribed,
he meets with inſurmountable obſtacles in
extending himſelf over an uncultivated
country. Even his gold affords him not
its uſual reſources in the neighbouring diſ-
tricts, nor is there a poſſibility of any ſup-
plies, but what muſt neceſſarily croſs the
ſeas. The irkſomeneſs of an impriſonment
of nine months duration, determined him
to regain New York by way of the Jerſeys;
and under the command of Clinton, ſuc-
ceſſor to Howe, this long and dangerous retreat was effected, without ſuſtaining ſo
much loſs as a more experienced enemy
would have occaſioned.

While the Engliſh were waſting away
their time in Penſylvania, an important
ſcene opens itſelf in the more northern part
of America. In the month of May, 1776,
Carleton had driven the provincials out of
Canada, and in October deſtroyed the
armed ſloops which they had conſtructed
on the Lake Champlain. This ſucceſs
drew Burgoyne to Ticonderago, in the
month of July in the following year. At
his

4

his approach, a garrifon, confifting of four
thoufand men, abandoned this important
poft, with the lofs of their rear-guard,
their artillery, and ammunition.

The Englifh general was naturally prefumptuous. A weaknefs fo extraordinary
increafed his arrogance. He had conceived
the defign of reuniting the troops of Canada
with thofe of New York by Hudfon's-bay.
This project was bold and great. Had he
fucceeded he would have cut North America in two, and, perhaps, have ended the
war. But, to have had fuccefs, it would
have been neceffary, that whilft one army
was going down, the other fhould have gone
up, the river. Having failed in this idea,
Burgoyne ought to have feen, from the
very firft fteps of it, that his enterprize was
chimerical. At every march it became
more and more fo. His communications
grew more diftant; his provifions lefs abundant. The Americans, taking heart again,
affembled from all parts round him. At
length this unlucky body of men found
themfelves caught, on the 13th of October,
at Saratoga; and nations learned with afto-
nifhment,

nilhment, that fix thoufand of the belt difciplined troops of the old hemifphere, had
laid down their arms before the hufbandmen of the new, conducted by the fortunate Gates. Thofe who remembered that
the Swedes, under Charles the Twelfth,
till then invincible, had capitulated before
the Ruffians, yet uncivilized, did not ac-
cufe the Englifh troops, but only blamed
the imprudence of their general.

This event, fo decifive in the opinion of
our politicians, was of no greater confequence than that with which other actions,
lefs favourable to the American arms, had
been attended. After three years of fighting, maffacre, and devaftation, the ftate of
things was fcarcely changed from what it
had been a fortnight after the commence-
ment of hoftilities. Let us endeavour to
difcover the caufes of fo ftrange a fingu-
larity.

Great Britain, accuftomed to ftorms at
home, faw not at firft all the danger there
might be in the tempeft which was rifing
in her remote poffeffions. For a long time
her troops had been infulted at Bofton ; an
authority,

Why the Englifh did not fucceed in bringing the confederate provinces to fubmiffion.

authority, independent of hers, had been formed in the province of Maffachufet. The other colonies were making difpofitions to follow this example, had not the adminiftration taken thofe great objects into their ferious confideration. When they were laid before parliament, both houfes were filled with clamour; and much declamation followed, after much declamation that had gone before. The fenate of the nation decreed at laft, that the country which was rebellious to its decrees, fhould by force be made obedient: but this violent refolution was executed with the flownefs too frequent in ftates of freedom.

England thought, in general, that coafts without defence, that countries entirely open, could not refift her fleets and armies. It did not appear to her that this expedition could be of fufficient duration to give time to the peaceful hufbandmen of America to learn the art of war. It was forgotten that the climate, the rivers, the defiles, the fwamps, the want of provifion, in proportion as advances were made into the country, and an infinity of other natural obftruc-

tions,

tions, militating againſt a rapid progreſs
in a region three-fourths uncultivated,
ſhould have made a part of the calculation.

Succeſs was ſtill more retarded by the
influence of moral cauſes.

Great Britain is the region of party. Her
kings have generally ſeemed to be well
enough convinced of the neceſſity of leav-
ing public affairs to the management of the
prevailing faction, by which they were
conducted commonly with intelligence and
with vigour, becauſe the principal agents
of which it was compoſed were animated
by a common intereſt. Then, to public
ſpirit, which reigns more in England
than in any other government of Europe, was added the power of a faction,
and that ſpirit of party which moves men's
minds ſo powerfully, becauſe it is always
the effect of paſſion. To rid himſelf of
this reſtraint, George the Third compoſed
his council of detached, unconnected members. This innovation was not attended
with any very great inconveniences, as long
as events rolled round in their common
courſe. But as ſoon as a war with Ame-

I   rica

rica had complicated a machine, which
was not before too fimple, it was perceived
that it had neither that ftrength, nor that
union, which are fo neceffary for the execution of great affairs. The wheels, too
far afunder, wanted, as we may fay, a
centre of motion, and a common impulfe.
They went fluggifhly and precipitately, by
turns. The adminiftration too much re-
fembled that of an ordinary monarchy,
when the principle of action proceeds not
from the head of an intelligent and active
monarch, who brings together all the
fprings under his own hand. There was
no longer any integrity or wholenefs in
what was undertaken, nor was there more
of it in what was executed.

A miniftry, without harmony and concord, was expofed to the inceffantly re-
newed attacks of a body of enemies, united,
clofe, and firm. Its refolutions, be they
what they would, were fure to be combated
by reafoning or by ridicule. It was re
proached for having been fevere with the
diftant members of the ftate, as it would
have been reproached for having been too

2   tender

tender to them. Even they, who in parliament were the moſt outrageous againſt
the treatment which had been ſhewn to the
Americans; they who moſt encouraged
them to reſiſtance; they who, perhaps, ſe-
cretly ſent them ſuccour, were as averſe to
their independence as the very miniſters
whom they laboured, without ceaſing, to re-
move or vilify. Could the oppoſition
have ſucceeded in diſguſting the king with
his confidents, or have obtained the ſacri-
fice of them by the cry of the nation, the
projeĉt of ſubjugating America had ſtill
been followed, but with more dignity,
more force, and perhaps with meaſures
better planned. As the reduĉtion of the
revolted provinces was not to be their work,
they rather wiſhed that this immenſe part
of the Britiſh empire might be ſeparated
from it, than that it ſhould be reunited to
by any other hands than theirs.

The aĉtivity of the generals repaired not
the vice of theſe contrarieties, and the delays in conſequence. They indulged the
ſoldier with too long repoſe; they employed
in meditating, the time for aĉting; they

approached

approached new-raifed men with the pre
caution they would have taken before veteran troops. The Englifh, who have fo
much impetuofity in party, are of a cool
and calm character in other things. They
are to be agitated but by violent paffions.
When this fpring is wanting, they move.
flow enough to count their fteps. Then
they govern themfelves by the temper of
their mind, which, in general, if we except the arts of imagination and tafte, is,
in every thing elfe, methodical and wife.
In war, their valour never lofes fight of
principles, or leaves much to chance.
Rarely do they leave, either on their flanks,
or in their rear, any thing which may give
them trouble. This fyftem has its advan-.
tages, particularly in a clofe and narrow.
country, in a country fet thick with ftrong
holds and fortified towns. But in the prefent circumftances, and upon the vaft continent of America, againft a people who
fhould not have had time allowed them for
their being fortified, or inured to war, the
perfection of the art, perhaps, had been
to have forgot it, and to fubftitute, in its

ftead, the rapid and impetuous march, and
the mighty darings which at once aftonifh,
ftrike, and overcome. It was in the firft
moments, above all, that it would have
been neceffary to imprefs upon the Americans, not the terror of fuch ravages as
affect a people, armed for their liberty,
more with indignation than with fear; but
that dread which is ftruck from a fuperiority
of talents and of arms, and which a war-
like people, of the old world, fhould naturally be fuppofed to carry to the new.
The confidence of victory had foon been
victory itfelf. But by too much circumfpection, by their too fervile attachment to
rules and principles, fkilful leaders failed
of rendering to their country the fervice it
expected from them, and which it was juftified in expecting.

The troops, on their fide, did not prefs
their commanders to lead them on. They
were juft come from a country, where the
caufe which had fent them acrofs the ocean,
made no impreffion. It was, in the eyes
of the people, but a broil which could not
be of any confequence. They confounded
the

the debates it occafioned in parliament with
other debates, often of fmall importance.
It was not talked of ; or if fome perfons
entertained themfelves with it, they were
not more earneft about it than about
thofe pieces of news, which, in great cities, occupy the idlenefs of every day.
The indifference of the nation had com-
municated itfelf to the defenders of its
rights. They would even have been afraid,
perhaps, to gain too decifive advantages
over countrymen, who had taken arms but
to keep themfelves from chains. In all the
monarchies of Europe, the foldier is but
an inftrument of defpotifm, and has its difpofition. He looks upon himfelf as belonging to the throne, and not to the country ; and a hundred thoufand armed men,
are but a hundred thoufand difciplined and
formidable flaves. The habit even of exer-
cifing the empire of force, that empire to
which all gives way, contributes to extin-
guifh in them every fpark of the love of
liberty. At length, the military government and fubordination, which moves thou-
fands of arms by a fingle voice, which
permits

permits no asking, nor seeing, nor judging, nor thinking; and, at the first signal, makes it a law to kill or die, compleats the work of changing these sentiments into principles, which make what may be called the morals of their state. It is not so in England. The influence of the constitution is so great, that it extends itself even to the troops. There, a man is a citizen before he is a soldier. Public opinion, conforming itself to the constitution, honours one, and lightly regards the other, of these titles. Thus we see by the history of the revolutions and tempests by which that turbulent island has been torn, that the English soldier, tho' enlisted for life, preserves for political liberty a passion, of which an idea is not easily to be formed in our countries of slaves.

How should the ardour which was wanting in the British troops have animated the Hessians, the Brunswickers, and the other Germans ranking under the same banners, all equally discontented with the princes who had sold them, discontented with the sovereign who had bought them, discon-

tented

tented with the nation which paid their wages, and difcontented with their comrades, who treated their mercenarinefs with contempt ? Befides, they had alfo brothers in the enemy's camp, to whom they dreaded to give death, and from whofe hand a wound would have grieved them with a double pain.

The fpirit of the Englifh army had been altered too, in confequence of a revolution in the manners of their country, which had taken place about fifteen or eighteen years before. The fucceffes of the laft war ; the extenfion which the peace had given to commerce ; the great acquifitions made in the Eaft Indies : all thefe means of fortune had, without interruption, accumulated in Great Britain prodigious riches. Thefe riches kindled the defire of new enjoyments. The great went to acquire them in foreign countries, and, above all, in France ; and brought home the poifon to their country. From the higher conditions, it flowed down into all the claffes, even to the loweft. To a character of plainnefs, fimplicity, referve, and haughtinefs, fucceeded a tafte for ex-
terior

terior fhew, for diffipation, gallantry, and
what is called politenefs. Travellers who
had formerly vifited this ifland fo renowned,
thought themfelves in another climate.
The contagion had fpread to the troops.
They carried with them to the new hemifphere the paffion which they had con-
tracted in the old, for gaming, for foft
accommodation, and good living. In de-
parting from their coaft, they fhould have
renounced the fuperfluities of which they
were enamoured. This tafte for luxury, this
ardour, fo much the more violent as it was
new, did not encourage them to purfue,
into the interior part of the country, an
enemy ever ready to plunge into it for
fhelter. Ye new politicians who advance
with fo much confidence that manners have
no influence on the fate of nations, that,
with regard to them, the meafure of greatnefs is that of riches; that the pleafures of
peace and the voluptuoufnefs of the citizen
cannot weaken the effect of thofe great
machines called armies, and of which the
European difcipline has, according to your
account, fo perfected the infallible and
tremendous

tremendous operations : you, who to fupport your opinion, muft turn away your
eyes from the afhes of Carthage and the
ruins of Rome, upon the recital I am making to you, fufpend your judgment, and
believe it poffible that there may be opportunities of fuccefs which are loft by
luxury. Believe, that, even to courageous
troops, independence on wants has been
often the chief caufe of conqueft. It is
too eafy perhaps to brave only death. For
nations corrupted by opulence a feverer
trial is referved, that of fupporting the lofs
of their pleafures.

Add to all thefe reafons, that the means
of war feldom arrived, acrofs fuch a length
of fea, in the convenient feafon for action.
Add, that the councils of George the
Third were wifely determined to have too
much influence in military operations which
were to be executed at fuch a diftance from
them ; and you will know the greateft part
of the obftacles by which the ruinous efforts of the mother-country againft the
freedom of her colonies were oppofed.

But

But how happened it that America did
not herfelf repulfe from her fhores thefe
Europeans who were bringing to her chains
or death ?

Why the confederate provinces did not fuc-ceed in driv-ing the Eng-lifh from the continent of America.

This new world was defended by regular troops, which at firft had been enlifted·
but for three or fix months, and afterwards
for three years, or as long as hoftilities
might continue. It was defended by citizens who took the field only when their
particular province was invaded or menaced. Neither this army always on foot,
nor this militia cafually affembled, had
a military turn. They were farmers,
traders, lawyers, exercifed only in the arts
of peace, and conducted to danger by
guides as little verfed as their fubalterns in
the very complicated fcience of war. In
this ftate of things, what hope could they
have of meafuring themfelves with advantage againft veterans in difcipline, formed
to evolutions, inftructed in tactics, and
abundantly provided with all the inftruments neceffary to a vigorous attack, to
an obftinate defence ?

Enthufiafm

Enthufiafm alone might have furmount-
ed thefe difficulties: but did there in
reality exift more enthufiafm in the colonies than in the mother-country ?

The general opinion in England, was,
that the parliament had effentially the right
of taxing every country which made a part
of the Britifh empire. Perhaps, in the
beginning of the troubles, not a hundred
individuals were to be found who would
have called this authority in queftion. Yet
no anger was excited by the refufal of the
Americans to acknowledge it. No hatred
was borne towards them, even after they
had taken arms in fupport of their pretenfions. As the labours of the people in the
interior part of the kingdom were not af-
fected by it, as the ftorm murmured but
at diftance, every one was peaceably occupied with his bufinefs, or gave himfelf up
without difturbance to his pleafures. They
all waited for the conclufion of the drama
without impatience, as if already certain
of what was to be exhibited in the unra-
velling of the plot.

The

The ferment muſt be ſuppoſed to have ſhewn itſelf at firſt much greater in the new hemiſphere than the old. Is ever the odious name of tyranny, or the grateful ſound of independance, pronounced to nations without communicating to them that warmth which produces motion? But did that warmth ſuſtain itſelf? Had the firſt vehemence of imagination laſted, muſt not the repreſſing of exceſſes have occupied the attention of the new authority? But ſo far from having cauſe to withhold courage, it had cowardice to purſue. It was ſeen to puniſh deſertion with death, ſtaining the ſtandard of liberty with blood. It was ſeen to refuſe admitting of an exchange of priſoners, for fear of augmenting the inclination of the troops to ſurrender at the firſt ſummons. It was ſeen reduced to the neceſſity of erecting tribunals for the proſecution of the generals or their lieutenants who ſhould too eaſily give up the poſts which their vigilance was to guard. It is true, that a hoary patriot, of fourſcore years, who was deſired to return to his fire ſide, cried out, *My death will be*

of

of ufe ; I fhall fhield with my body a younger man. It is true, that Putnam faid to a royalift his prifoner, *Return to thy commander, and if he afks thee how many troops I have, tell him, that I have enough ; that, even if he fhould beat them, I fhould have ftill enough ; and that he will find, in the event, that I have too many for him and for the tyrants whom he ferves.* Thefe fentiments were heroic, but they were rare ; and they became lefs common every day.

The intoxication was never general ; and it could be but momentaneous. None of thofe energetic caufes, which have produced fo many revolutions upon the globe, exifted in North America. Neither religion nor laws had there been outraged. The blood of martyrs or patriots had not there ftreamed from fcaffolds. Morals had not been there infulted. Manners, cuftoms, habits, no object dear to nations had there been the fport of ridicule. Arbitrary power had not there torn any inhabitant from the arms of his family and his friends, to drag him to a dreary dungeon. Public order had not been there inverted. The

principles

principles of adminiſtration had not been
changed there; and the maxims of government had there always remained the
fame. The whole queſtion was reduced
to the knowing whether the mother country
had, or had not, the right to lay, directly,
or indirectly, a ſlight tax upon the colonies: for the accumulated grievances in
the manifeſto were valid only in conſequence of this leading grievance. This,
almoſt metaphyſical, queſtion was ſcarcely
of ſufficient importance to cauſe the multitude to riſe, or at leaſt to intereſt them
ſtrongly in a quarrel for which they ſaw
their land deprived of the hands deſtined
to its cultivation, their harveſts laid waſte,
their fields covered with the dead bodies
of their kindred, or ſtained with their own
blood. To theſe calamities, the work of
the royal troops upon the coaſt, were ſoon
added more inſupportable ones in the heart
of the country.

Never had the reſtleſſneſs of the courts
of London and Verſailles diſturbed the
tranquillity of North America but both
theſe powers brought ſome of the migra-
tory

tory clans in this part of the new hemifphere to partake in their fanguinary ftrife.
Inftructed by experience in the weight
which thefe hordes could add to the fcale,
the Englifh and the colonifts were equally
refolved to employ them for their mutual
deftruction.

Carleton tried, firft, to arm thefe barbarous hands in Canada. " It is the dif-
" pute," faid they in anfwer to his folici-
tations, " of a father with his children;
" we do not think it right for us to enter
" into this domeftic fquabble."—" But
" if the rebels fhould come to attack this
" province, would not you help us to
" drive them back?"—" Ever fince the
" peace the hatchet of war has been bu-
" ried forty fathoms deep."—" You
" would certainly find it, if you were to
" dig for it."—" The helve of it is rot-
" ten, and we cannot make any ufe of it."

The United States were not more fortunate. " We have heard talk of fome
" differences that have happened between
" Old and New England (faid the tribe
" of the Oneidas to their deputies) but
" we

" we fhall never take a part in fuch atro-
" cious divifions. War between brethren
" is a ftrange and a new thing in thefe re-
" gions. Our traditions have left us no
" example of this nature. Supprefs your
" mad hatred ; and may a benevolent fun
" difperfe the black vapour in which you
" are involved !"

The Mafphies alone feemed to intereft
themfelves in the caufe of the Americans.
" There, (faid thefe good favages to them)
" there's fixteen fhillings for you. 'Tis
" all that we have. We thought to have
" bought fome rum with it; we'll drink
" water. We'll go a hunting. If any
" beafts fall by our arrows, we'll fell their
" fkins, and bring you the money."

But in time, the very active agents of
Great-Britain fucceeded in conciliating to it
many nations of thefe aborigines. Its interefts were preferred to thofe of its enemies, as well becaufe the remoter diftance
had prevented the favages from having received fo many outrages from it as from
their proud neighbours, as becaufe it could
and would better pay the fervices which

K   might

might be rendered to its caufe. Under its banners, thefe allies, whofe characteriftic fiercenefs knew no reftraint, did a hundred times more damage to the colonifts fettled near the mountains, than had been fuffered, from the royal troops, by thofe of their fellow citizens whom a happier deftiny had fixed upon the confines of the ocean.

Thefe calamities attacked but a more or lefs confiderable number of the members of the United States, who foon after were all, collectively, afflicted by an inward hurt.

The metals, which, throughout the whole globe, reprefent all the objects of commerce, had, in this part of the new-world, never been abundant. The fmall quantity of them which had been feen there, difappeared even at the commence-ment of hoftilities. To thefe figns, uni-verfally agreed upon, were fubftituted figns peculiar to thefe provinces. ·Paper re-placed filver and gold. In order to give fome dignity to the new pledge, it was adorned with emblems, which might con-tinually remind the people of the greatnefs

nefs of their undertaking, of the ineftim-
able price of liberty, and of the neceffity
of a perfeverance fuperior to all fufferings.
The artifice did not fucceed. Thefe ideal
riches were rejected. The more the mul-
tiplication of them was urged by want, the
greater did their depreciation grow. The
congrefs was indignant at the affronts given
to its money, and declared all thofe to be
traitors to their country who fhould not
receive it as they would have received gold
itfelf.

Did not this body know, that prepof-
feffions are no more to be controled than
feelings are? Did it not perceive,
that in the prefent crifis every rational man
would be afraid of expofing his fortune?
Did it not fee, that at the beginning of a
republic it permitted to itfelf the exercife
of fuch acts of defpotifm as are unknown
even in the countries which are moulded
to, and become familiar with, fervitude
and oppreffion? Could it pretend that it
did not punifh a want of confidence with
the pains which would have been fcarcely
merited by revolt and treafon? Of all

this

this was the congrefs well aware. But it had no choice of means. It's defpifed and defpicable fcraps of paper were actually thirty times below their original value, when more of them were ordered to be made. On the 13th of September, 1779, there was of this paper money, amongft the public, to the amount of £35,544,155. The ftate owed moreover £8,385,356, without reckoning the particular debts of fingle provinces.

The people had no amends for this do-meftic fcourge, as it might be called, by an eafy communication with all the other parts of the world. Great Britain had in-tercepted their navigation with Europe, with the Weft Indies, with all the latitudes which their veffels covered. Then, they faid to the univerfe, " It is the Englifh " name which makes us odious; we fo- " lemnly abjure it. All men are our " brethren. We are the friends of all " nations. Every flag may, without fear " of infult, fhew itfelf upon our coafts, " frequent our ports. An invitation, fo " feducing in appearance, was not com-
" plied

plied with. Thofe ftates which are truly commercial ones, knowing that North America had been reduced to contract debts at the epoch even of her greateft profperity, thought wifely that in her prefent diftrefs fhe would be able to pay but very little for what might be carried to her. The French alone, who dare every thing, dared to brave the inconveniences of this new connection. But by the judicious vigilance of Admiral Lord Howe, the greateft part of the fhips which they fent out were taken before they arrived at the places of their deftination, and the others at their departure from the American coafts. Of many hundreds of veffels which failed from France, but twenty-five or thirty returned back to it, and even thofe brought no profit, or very little, to their owners.

A multitude of privations, added to fo many other misfortunes, might make the Americans regret their former tranquillity, and incline them to an accommodation with England. In vain had the people been bound to the new government by

K 3   the

the facredness of oaths and the influence
of religion. In vain had endeavours been
ufed to convince them that it was impoffible to treat fafely with a country in which
one parliament might overturn what fhould
have been eftablifhed by another. In vain
had they been threatened with the eternal
refentment of an exafperated and vindictive
enemy. It was poffible that thefe diftant
troubles might not be balanced by the
weight of prefent evils.

So thought the Britifh miniftry, when
they fent to the New-world public agents,
authorized to offer every thing except independence to thefe very Americans, from
whom they had two years before exacted
an unconditional fubmiffion. It is not im-
probable but that by this plan of conciliation, a few months fooner, fome effect
might have been produced. But at the
period at which it was propofed by the
Court of London, it was rejected with
difdain, becaufe this meafure appeared but
as an argument of fear and weaknefs.
The people were already re-affured. The
congrefs, the generals, the troops, the bold
and

and fkilful men who in each colony had poffeffed themfelves of the authority; every thing had recovered its firft fpirit. This was the effect of a treaty of friend-fhip and commerce between the United States and the Court of Verfailles, figned the 6th of February, 1778.

If the Britifh miniftry had reflected up-on it, they would have comprehended that the fame delirium which was drawing them to attack their colonies was reducing them to the neceffity of declaring war in the fame inftant againft France. Then pre-vailed in the councils of this crown the circumfpection which muft always be in-fpired by a new reign. Then the finances were ftill in the confufion into which they had been plunged by a madnefs of twenty years. Then the decayed condition of the navy was fuch as filled every citizen with difquiet. Then Spain, already fatigued with her extravagant expedition of Algiers, found herfelf in embarraffments which would not have permitted her to run to the fuccour of her ally. And then might England, without rafhnefs, have promifed

France ac-knowleges the indepen-dence of the United States. This meafure oc-cafions the war between this crown and that of England.

K 4 herfelf

herself fuccefs againft the moft powerfu
of her enemies, and to intimidate America
by victories gained or conquefts made near
home. The importance that it was of,
for this crown to take away from its rebellious fubjects the only fupport of which
they might be affured, would have dimi-
nifhed the indignation infpired by a viola-
tion of the moft folemn treaties.

George the Third faw nothing of all
this. The obfcure fuccours which the
Court of Verfailles fent to the provinces
armed for the defence of their rights, did
not open his eyes. The dock-yards of
France were filling with fhipwrights. Her
arfenals were filling with artillery. Scarcely
was there room remaining in her magazines
for more naval ftores. Her ports prefented
the moft menacing appearance ; and this
ftrange blindnefs ftill continued. To
awaken the Court of St. James's from its
lethargy, it was neceffary that Lewis the
Sixteenth fhould fignify to it, on the 14th
of March, that he had acknowledged the
independence of the United States.

This

This fignification was a declaration of
war. It was impoffible that a nation, more
accuftomed to give provocation than receive it, could patiently look on, whilft
another nation was loofening it's fubjects
from their bonds of allegiance, and raifing
them up with much parade to the rank of
fovereign powers. All Europe forefaw that
two ftates, in rivalfhip for ages, were about
to tinge the waters of the ocean with their
blood, and again play that dreadful game,
in which public profperities will never
compenfate for particular difafters. They
in whom ambition had not extinguifhed all
benevolence for their fellow-creatures, de-
plored beforehand the calamities, which,
in either hemifphere, were ready to fall
upon the human race.

The bloody fcene, notwithftanding, did
not open yet ; and this delay gave credulity a ground of hope, that peace would
ftill continue. It was not known that a
fleet, which had failed from Toulon, was
commiffioned to attack the Englifh in
North America. It was not known that
orders had been difpatched from London
to

to drive the French from the Eaft Indies.
Without being initiated in thofe myfteries
of perfidy, which infidious politics are arrived at regarding as great ftrokes of ftate,
judicious men fuppofed that hoftilities muft
be inevitable, and on the point of taking
place, even in our ocean. This event,
which had been forefeen, was brought on
by the fight of two frigates, on the 17th
of June, 1778.

Here our tafk becomes more and more
difficult. Our fole object is to be ufeful,
and to be true. Far be from us that fpirit
of party which blinds and degrades thofe
who are the conductors, and thofe who
afpire to be the inftructors, of mankind.
Our wifh is for our country; our homage
is to juftice. We honour virtue, in whatever place, in whatever form, fhe is feen:
the diftinctions of condition and of nation
cannot eftrange us from her; and the man
who is juft and magnanimous is our countryman over all the world. If in the different events which pafs under our eyes, we
blame with boldnefs what appears to us
blame-worthy, we feek not the vain and
forry

forry pleafure of cafting indifcreet reproach.
But we are fpeaking to nations and to pofterity. We ought faithfully to tranfmit to
them what may be influential on the public
good. We ought to give them the hiftory
of errors, to teach them how they may be
fhunned. Should we dare to be traiteroufly
wanting to fo great a duty, we might, perhaps, flatter the generation which paffeth
away; but truth and juftice, which are
eternal, would impeach us to future generations, who would read us with contempt,
and pronounce not our name but with difdain. In this long career we fhall be juft
to thofe who ftill exift, as we have been to
thofe who exift no more. If, amongft the
men of power, there are any who are offended at this freedom, let us not fear to
tell them, that we are but the organ of a
fupreme tribunal, which reafon is erecting
upon a bafis that cannot be fhaken. There
is no longer a government in Europe but
fhould ftand in fear of its determinations.
Public opinion, which is becoming more
and more informed, and which nothing has
power to arreft or awe, has its eyes open
upon

upon nations and their courts. It pene-
trates into the cabinets where policy would
lie hid. There it judges the depofitaries
of power, their weaknesses and their
paffions; and, by the empire of genius
and knowledge, raifes itfelf, on all fides,
above the minifters of kings, to incite or
to reftrain them. Woe to them who de-
fpife or brave it ! This feeming courage is
weaknefs in reality. Woe to them whofe
talents cannot arm them with a confidence
to fuftain its look ! Let fuch, that they
may once do juftice, at leaft to themfelves,
lay down the burden too heavy for their feeble fhoulders. They will ceafe to expofe
themfelves and the nations they pretend
to ferve.

France began the war with invaluable
advantages. The time, the place, the circumftances; fhe had chofen all. It was
not till after fhe had, at leifure, made her
preparations, till after fhe had increafed
her power to the proper pitch, that fhe
fhewed herfelf upon the field of battle. She
had to combat but an enemy who was
humbled,

humbled, weakened, and difcouraged by
domeſtic feuds. The wiſhes of other nations were with her, againſt thoſe impe-
rious maſters, or, as they were called,
thoſe tyrants of the ocean.

Events ſeemed to correſpond to the defire of Europe. The French officers, who
had old humiliations to wipe away, performed brilliant actions, the remembrance
of which will be of long duration. Great
theoretic knowledge, and unſhaken courage, ſupplied what might be wanting in
them from practice and experience. All
the ſingle engagements, of ſhip to ſhip,
did them the higheſt honour, and moſt of
them terminated to their advantage. The
Britiſh fleet ran ſtill greater danger than the
iſolated veſſels. It was ſo roughly treated
as to have cauſe to fear being wholly or
partially deſtroyed; had not the French
fleet, by which it was reduced, off Uſhant,
to this almoſt deſpairing ſtate, been deftined, from timid orders, from odious
intrigues, from the weakneſs of its admirals, or from all theſe motives together,

ther, to quit the fea and be the firſt to make for port.

In the intoxication of this, perhaps, unexpected fuccefs, France feemed to lofe fight of her deareſt intereſts. Her principal object ſhould have been to intercept the commerce of her enemies, cutting the double nerve of their ſtrength, their feamen and their wealth, and fo fap, at once, the two foundations of Engliſh greatnefs. Nothing was more eafy for a power prepared a long while for hoſtilities, than to intercept fleets of merchantmen, quite unprepared, and very feebly convoyed. This was not done. The immenfe riches expected by Great Britain, from all parts of the globe, entered peaceably into her harbours, without fuffering the fmalleſt diminution.

The commerce of France, on the contrary, was harraffed in both the hemifpheres, and every where intercepted. Her colonies faw raviſhed from them, on their very coaſts, fubfiftences, to welcome which they were reaching out their arms with

all

all the eagernefs of want; whilft the mother-
country was deprived of four millions fterling, arrived almoft in her fight. This
reverfe was not without a caufe. Let us
endeavour to difcover it.

The French navy had been a long time
unfuccefsful; and it was to the vice of its
conftitution that fo many misfortunes had
been afcribed. Many attempts had been
made to modify or change the regulations
of it; but thefe innovations, good or bad,
were always repelled with a more or lefs
ftrongly marked difdain. At length its
admirals dictated themfelves, in 1776, a
difpofition, which rendering them abfolute
mafters of the roads or anchoring-places,
of the arfenals, of the dock-yards, and
the magazines, deftroyed that mutual in-
fpectorfhip, which Lewis the Fourteenth
thought it was right he fhould eftablifh,
between the military officers and thofe of
the adminiftration. From that time there
was no longer any refponfibility, regula-
tion, or œconomy in the ports. Every
thing there fell into diforder and confufion.

The

The new plan had an influence that was ftill more unhappy. Till this period it was the miniftry who had directed the naval operations towards the end aimed at by their politics. This authority paffed, perhaps, almoft without being perceived, to thofe who were to execute thefe operations, which took infenfibly a tincture from their prejudices. Thefe prejudices inclined them to think, that it was not in heavily and laborioufly convoying the fhips of their nation, or in remaining out upon difficult cruizes, to furprize or deftroy thofe of the enemy's nation, that fame was to be acquired. This double duty, therefore, was entirely neglected, or very ill performed, in confequence of the opinion common at Breft, that fuch a fervice had nothing noble in it, and led not to any kind of glory.

It muft be confeffed, that this prejudice is a very odd one, and quite contrary to all the laws of fociety. What can be fuppofed to have been the defign of ftates in inftituting this military force deftined to

fcour

scour the seas? Was it only to procure
promotions for those who command or
serve? Only to give them opportunities of
exercising a valour useless to every body but
themselves? Only to stain red another ele-
ment with bloody battles? No, undoubtedly. Fleets of war upon the ocean, are
what fortresses and ramparts are for inhabitants of cities; what the national armies
are for provinces exposed to incursions of
the foe. There are some forts of property
attached to the soil; there are others which
are created, transported by commerce, and,
as they may be called, wandering on the
ocean. Both these forts of property want
defenders. Warriors, that is your function. What would be said, if the land-forces
should refuse to protect the inhabitants
of cities, the cultivaters of fields, and to
drive back the fire threatened to the harvest?
Naval officers, you think yourselves debased
by convoying and protecting commerce.
But if commerce is to be no more protected,
what will become of the riches of the state,
of which, without doubt, you expect a

L   part,

part, in recompence of your fervice? What will become of your own property, in the revenue of your land, which commerce and the circulation of wealth chiefly contribute to make fruitful? You think yourfelves debafed. What, debafed in making yourfelf ufeful to your countrymen! And what are all the orders in the ftate, to whom government has committed any portion of the public power, but protectors and defenders of your countrymen and their wealth? Your poft is upon the ocean, as that of the magiftrate upon the bench, that of the foldier in the camp, and that of the monarch himfelf upon the throne, where he commands from a higher ftation but to take a wider furvey, and comprize, at one view, all thofe who ftand in need of his protection and defence. Know that glory is to be gleaned in every field on which a fervice to your country can be performed. Know, that to preferve is more glorious, as well as more bleffed, than to deftroy. In ancient Rome there were alfo admirers of glory. Yet, there, the glory of having faved a fingle citizen,

was

was preferred to the glory of having flain
a hoft of foes. What, fee you not that in
faving the commercial fhips, you fave the
fortune of the ftate? Yes, your valour is
fplendid; it is known to Europe as well as
to your country; but what boots it to your
countrymen, that it has been difplayed
upon occafions of eclat, that it has brought
the fhip of your enemy in tow, or blown
its ruins wide upon the waves, if you have
fuffered to perifh, or be taken, the fhips
which bear your country's riches; if in the
very port, which you triumphantly re-
enter, a thoufand defolate families deplore
their fortunes loft? On your landing, inftead of hearing the fhouts of victory, you
will be received with filence and dejection;
and your exploits will be deftined but to
fwell the recital of a court-gazette, and
thofe public papers, which, in amufing
idlenefs, give glory but for a day, when
that glory is not graven upon the hearts of
your fellow citizens, by the remembrance
of real utility to the common good.

The maxims facred at Portfmouth were
very different. There was felt, there was

refpected.

reſpected, the dignity of commerce. There
it was both a duty and an honour to defend
it; and events have decided on which ſide
the naval officers had the juſteſt ideas of
their function.

Great Britain had juſt experienced a very
humiliating reverſe in the new world, and
a more powerful enemy threatened her with
greater diſaſters in the old. This alarming
ſituation filled all minds with doubtfulneſs
and diſtruſt. The national riches arrive.
Thoſe of the rival power add to the enor-
mous maſs; and inſtantly public credit is
reanimated; hope ſprings up again, and this
people, who were contemptuouſly thought
to be brought down, reſume, and ſuſtain,
their uſual proweſs and their uſual pride.

The ports of France, on the contrary,
are filled with groans. A ſhameful and
ruinous inaction ſucceeded to an activity
which contributed to their fame and riches.
The indignation of the merchants commu-
nicated itſelf to all the nation. The firſt
moments of ſucceſs are moments of intoxication, in which faults ſeem to be juſ-
tified as well as hid. But misfortune gives
more

more feverity to judgement. The nation then obferves more nearly thofe who govern, and loudly calls for an account of the employment of the power and authority which have been committed to them. The councils of Lewis the Sixteenth are reproached, for having wounded the majefty of the firft power on the globe, in difavowing, to the face of the univerfe, the fuccours which were fent continually to the Americans in a clandeftine manner. They are reproached, for having, by a minifterial intrigue, or, by the afcendancy of fome obfcure agents, engaged the nation in a difaftrous war, whilft they fhould have been occupied in putting the fprings of government again in order, in healing the tedious wounds of a reign, of which the latter half was divided between depredation and fhame, between the bafenefs of vice and the convulfions of defpotifm. They are reproached, for having provoked the conteft by infidious politics, for having defcended to wrap themfelves round with guile, in difcourfes unworthy of France; for having employed with England the lan-

L 3   guage

guage of a timid audacity, which feems
to difown and contradict, the projects which
are formed, and the fentiments which are
uppermoft, in the heart; a language which
can only debafe him from whom it proceeds, without deceiving him to whom it
is addreffed; and, whilft it brings difhonour, can make that difhonour of no ufe
either to the minifter or to the ftate. How
much nobler had it been to fay, with all
the franknefs of dignity; " Englifhmen,
" you have abufed your victories. Now
" is the moment for you to fhew juftice;
" or it fhall be that of vengeance. Europe
" is weary of fuffering tyrants. She re-
" enters at length upon her rights. Hence-
" forward, equality or war. Chufe." It
is thus that they would have been talked
to by that Richelieu, whom every citizen,
it is true, fhould hate, becaufe he was an
inhuman butcher, and, that he might reign
defpotic, murdered his enemies with the
hangman's axe; but whom, as a minifter,
the nation is bound to honour, as it was
he who firft fhewed France her dignity,
and gave her, amongft the ftates of Europe,

rope, the air which became her power. It is thus that they would have been talked to by that Lewis, who, for forty years together, knew how to be worthy of the age to which he gave a name, who mixed greatnefs with his very faults, who never, even in adverfity and abafement, degraded his people or himfelf. Ah, for governing a great nation, a great character is requifite. There is no fitnefs for it in thofe minds which are indifferent and cold from levity, to which abfolute authority is but as it were a kind of laft amufement, which carelefsly leave great interefts floating at the caprice of chance, and are more occupied in preferving than employing power. Why, it is afked again, why did men, who hold in their hands all the authority of the ftate, and have but to command in order to be obeyed, why did they fuffer themfelves to be prevented, in all feas, by an enemy whofe conftitution muft of neceffity caufe flownefs in putting their meafures in execution? Why did they, by an inconfiderate treaty, tie themfelves down to conditions with the Congrefs, which they might

L 4   themfelves

themfelves have held in dependence, by
ample and regular fupplies ? Why, in
fhort, did they not ftrengthen and confirm
the revolution, by keeping always, on the
northern coafts of the new world, a fqua-
dron which might protect the colonies,
and, at the fame time, make our alliance
to be refpected ? But Europe, who has
her eyes fixed upon us, fees a great defign,
and no concerted meafures ; fees, in our
arfenals and our ports, immenfe preparations, and no execution ; fees menacing
fleets fitted out, and the pompous expence
of them rendered almoft ufelefs ; fees fpirit
and valour in fubalterns, irrefolution and
timidity in chiefs ; fees whatever proclaims,
on one hand, the ftrength and the awe-
commanding power of a great people,
and, on the other, the flacknefs and
weaknefs infeparable from its character
and views. It is by this ftriking contradiction between our projects and their
execution, between our means and their
direction, that the genius of England,
ftunned for a moment, has refumed his
vigour ; and it is even now a problem for
Europe

Europe to refolve, if, in declaring for America, we have not ourfelves revived and advanced the Englifh power.

Such are the complaints with which all parts of the kingdom ring, and which we are not afraid to collect together here, and lay before the eyes of authority, if it deigns to read or hear them.

In fhort, philofophy, whofe firft fentiment is the defire to fee all governments juft and all people happy, in cafting her eyes upon this alliance of a monarchy with a people who are defending their liberty, is curious to know its motive. She fees at once, too clearly, that the happinefs of mankind has no part in it. She thinks that if the Court of Verfailles had been determined by the love of juftice, it would have fettled in the firft article of its agreement with America, *that all oppreffed people have the right of refifting their oppreffors.* But this maxim, which forms one of the laws of England; which a king of Hungary was great enough, when he was afcending the throne, to make one of the conftitutions of the ftate; which was

adopted

adopted by one of the greateſt princes who
reigned over the world, Trajan, when he
ſaid, before an aſſembly of the Roman people, to the firſt officer of the empire, in
preſenting him with a drawn ſword, according to cuſtom upon inveſting him with
his charge, *Uſe it for me, if I continue juſt* ;
againſt me, if I become tyrannical. This
maxim is too foreign for our feeble and
corrupted governments, in which the ſuf-
fering patiently is ſo much become a duty,
that the ſufferer ought to deprecate a ſen-
ſation of his miſery, leſt it be puniſhed as
a crime.

But the moſt bitter complaints are directed bove all to Spain. She is blamed
for her blindneſs, her wavering, her tardi-
neſs, and ſometimes even for her infidelity:
all which accuſations are ill-founded.

Some politicians imagined, in ſeeing
France engage herſelf without neceſſity in
a naval war, that this crown ſuppoſed itſelf
powerful enough to divide the Britiſh domain, without ſharing with an ally the
honour of this important revolution. We
ſhall not examine whether the ſpirit which
then

then reigned in the cabinet of Verfailles authorifed this conjecture. It is now known that this crown, which from the very beginning of the troubles had fent fecret fuccour to the Americans, was watching for the propitious moment of declaring openly in their favour. The event of Saratoga appeared to it the moft favourable conjuncture for propofing to the Catholic king to make the caufe a common one. Whether it were that this prince might then judge the liberty of the United States to be contrary to his intereft ; whether the refolution might appear to him to be pre cipitate ; or whether, in fhort, other political objects might require all his attention, he did not agree to the propofal. From his character it was fuppofed that repeated folicitation would be ufelefs. After the firft experiment, he was fo little applied to about this great affair, that it was without his being apprifed of it that the Court of Verfailles caufed it to be fignified at St. James's that it had acknowledged the independence of the confederate provinces.

In

In the mean time the land and sea forces which Spain employed against the Portuguese in the Brazils were returned home. The rich fleet which she expected from Mexico was arrived in her ports. The treasures which came to her from Peru and from her other possessions were secure. She was free from all inquietude, and mistress of her motions, when she aspired to the glory of being a pacificator between the two hemispheres. Her mediation was accepted, as well by France, whose bold attempts had not been attended with the happy consequences which she had promised herself from them, as by England, who might fear the having an additional adversary to contend with.

Spain, not having succeeded in reconciling England and France, declares for the latter power. Charles the Third sustained with dignity the great part he had to act. He awarded that, laying down their arms, each of the belligerant powers should be maintained in the territories which it should occupy at the time of the convention; that a congress should be formed, in which the different pretensions should be discussed; and that no fresh hostilities should commence 'till

'till after the expiration of a twelve-month's notice.

This monarch was aware that this arrangement gave to Great Britain a facility of being reconciled with her colonies, or at least of making them purchase, by great advantages to her commerce, the ports which she occupied in the midst of them. He was aware that it must wound the dignity of the king his nephew, who had engaged to maintain the United States in the totality of their territory. But he would be just; and without forgetting all personal considerations one cannot be so.

This plan of conciliation was displeasing to Verfailles, whose only consolation was ministered by the hope that it would be rejected at London. This hope was not deceived. England could not resolve upon acknowledging the Americans to be really independant; though they were not to be called to the conferences which were to have taken place; though France could not negotiate for them; though their interests were to have been taken care of solely by a mediator who was not bound to them

by

by any treaty, and who, perhaps, at the
bottom of his heart, was not defirous of
their profperity; though her refufal threatened her with an enemy the more.

It is in fuch a circumftance as this; it
is in the time when noble pride elevates
the foul fuperior to all terror; when nothing is feen more dreadful than the fhame
of receiving the law, and when there is
no doubt or hefitation which to chufe
between ruin and difhonour; it is then,
that the greatnefs of a nation is difplayed.
I acknowledge however that men, accuftomed to judge of things by the event,
call great and perilous refolutions, heroifm
or madnefs, according to the good or bad
fuccefs with which they have been attended.
If then. I fhould be afked, what is the
names which fhall in years to come be
given to the firmnefs, which was in this
moment exhibited by the Englifh, I fhould
anfwer that I do not know. But that
which it deferves, I know. I know that
the annals of the world hold out to us
but rarely, the auguft and majeftic fpec-

tac e

tacle of a nation, which chufes rather to renounce its duration than its glory.

The Britifh miniftry had no fooner given their determination, than the Court of Madrid efpoufed the quarrel of that of Verfailles, and confequently that of the Americans. Spain had then fixty-three fhips of the line and fix on the ftocks. France had eighty of the line, and eight upon the ftocks. The United States had but twelve frigates; but a great number of privateers.

To all this united force England had to oppofe but ninety-five fhips of the line, with twenty-three upon the ftocks. The fixteen which were to be feen in her ports, over and above, were unfit for fervice, and had been converted into prifons or hofpitals. Inferior in inftruments of war, fhe was ftill more fo in means of all forts for their employment. Her domeftic diffenfions ftill weakened the refources which remained. It is the nature of governments truly free to be agitated during peace. It is by this inteftine motion that the fpirits preferve their energy and the continual remembrance

remembrance of the nation's rights. But
in war, all ferments ought to ceafe, all
hatreds to be extinguifhed, all interefts to
coalefce and be mutually fubfervient to
the public good. It happened quite otherwife, at this time, in the Britifh ifles.
Never were there more violent diffenfions.
Never did contrary pretenfions fhew themfelves in any circumftance with lefs referve. The public good was by either
faction audacioufly trodden under foot.
Thofe houfes of parliament, in which the
moft important queftions had formerly
been difcuffed with eloquence, with dignity, and with power, now rung but with
the clamours of rage, but with the groffeft
infults, but with altercations as hurtful
as they were indecent. The few true
friends of the nation who were remaining
called loudly for another Pitt, for the minifter who like him fhould have *neither
relations nor friends*; but this extraordinary man did not appear. And indeed it
was pretty generally imagined that this
people would now give way, notwithftanding
the high-fpiritednefs of its character, notwithftanding

withftanding the experience of its admirals, notwithftanding the bravery of its feamen, notwithftanding that energy which a free nation muft acquire from vibrating with concuffion;

But the empire of chance is a very wide one. Who knows in favour of which fide the elements fhall declare? By a guft of wind, is a victory given or fnatched away. The difcharge of a gun difconcerts a fleet by it admiral's death. Signals are not feen or heard; are not obeyed. Experience, valour, fkill, are thwarted by ignorance, by jealoufy, by treachery, by an affurance of impunity. A fog covers contending navies, and feparates or confounds them. A tempeft or a calm equally preferves, or equally deftroys. Forces are divided by the unequal celerity of fhips. The propitious moment is miffed, by pufillanimity which lingers, or by rafhnefs which rufhes on Plans fhall have been formed with wifdom; but their fuccefs fhall fail for want of concert in the movements of execution. By an inconfiderate order of the court,

M what

what might have proved a proud day, is decided to dishonour. Projects are changed by a minister's disgrace or death. Is it possible that a strict union should long subsist amongst confederates of characters so opposite, as the hasty, light, disdainful Frenchman, the jealous, haughty, sly, slow, circumspective Spaniard, and the American, who is secretly snatching looks at the mother-country, and would rejoice, were they compatible with his independence, at the disasters of his allies? Will these nations long delay, whether they act separately or conjointly, mutually to accuse, complain, and be embroiled? Ought not their greatest hope to be that multiplied ill-successes may do no more than replunge them into that humiliating state from which they endeavoured to emerge, and firmly fix the trident in the hand of England; whilst a considerable defeat or two would bring down this ambitious people from ever ranking again amongst the principal powers of the European world?

Who

Who shall decide then, who can fore-
see, the event? France and Spain united
have powerful means to employ; England, the art of employing her's. France
and Spain have their treasures; England,
a great national credit. On one side, the
multitude of men; on the other, the superiority in the art of working ships, and,
as it were, of subjecting the sea in fighting. Here, impetuosity and valour; there,
valour and experience. In one party, the
activity which absolute monarchy gives
to designs; in the other, the vigour and
elasticity which liberty supplies. There,
losses and grudges to revenge; here, their
late glory, with the sovereignty of America, and of the ocean, to recover and pre-
serve. The allied nations have the advantage with which the union of two vast
powers must be attended, but the inconvenience likewise which must result from
this very union, by the difficulty of harmony and concord both in their designs,
and in the execution of them by their
respective forces; England is abandoned
to herself, but having only her own forces

to

to direct, she has the advantage of unity
in designs, and of a more sure and perhaps
more ready disposition in ideas: she can
more easily range her plans of defence and
offence under a single view.

In order to weigh the matter with ex-
actness, we should yet put into the scales
the different energy which may be com-
municated to the rival nations by a war,
which is in a great many respects but a
war of kings and ministers on one side;
but, on the other, a truly national war, in
which the greatest interests of England are
concerned; that of a commerce which
produces her riches, that of an empire
and a glory on which her greatness rests.

In short, if we consider the spirit of the
French nation, opposite to that of the nation with which it is at variance, we shall
see that the ardour of the Frenchman is as
quickly extinguished as it is inflamed;
that he hopes every thing when he begins,
that he despairs of every thing as soon as
an obstacle shall retard him; that, from
his character, his arm must be nerved by
the enthusiasm of success, in order to reap

more

more fuccefs : that the Englifhman, on the contrary, lefs prefumptuous, notwithftanding his natural boldnefs, at the beginning, knows how, when occafions calls for it, to ftruggle courageoufly, to raife himfelf in proportion as the danger rifes, and to ga ther advantages even from difgrace : like the robuft oak to which Horace compares the Romans, which, mutilated by the axe, fprings afrefh under the ftrokes which are given it, and draws vigour and fpirit from its very loffes and its very wounds.

Hiftory fhews us likewife that few leagues have divided the fpoil of the na tion againft which they have been formed. Athens victorious over Perfia ; Rome faved from Hannibal ; in modern times, Venice efcaped from the famous league of Cambray ; and, even in our own days, Pruffia rendered by the genius of one man capable to cope with Europe, fhould fufpend our judgment upon the iffue of the prefent war.

But let us fuppofe that the houfe of Bourbon have the advantages with which

M 3   it

it may have been flattered. What ought
to be its conduct?

What
ought to be
the politics
of the house
of Bourbon,
if victori-
ous.

France is in all points of view the empire the moſt ſtrongly conſtituted, of which
any remembrance has been preſerved in
the annals of the world. Without being
able to bear any compariſon with her,
Spain is likewiſe a very powerful ſtate, and
her means of proſperity are continually
increaſing. The moſt important concern
then of the houſe of Bourbon ought to be,
to obtain pardon of its neighbours for the
advantages which it has from nature,
which it owes to art, or which have been
beſtowed on it by events. Should it endeavour to augment its ſuperiority, the
alarm would become general, and it would
be thought that an univerſal ſlavery was
threatened. It is perhaps to be wondered
at, that the other nations of Europe have
not yet thwarted it in its projects againſt
England. The reſentment which the in-
juſtice and the haughtıneſs of this proud
iſland have every where inſpired, muſt be
the cauſe of this inaction. But hatred is
ſilent when intereſt appears. It is poſſible
that

that Europe may think the weakening of Great Britain in the old and the new hemifphere contrary to its fafety; and that, after having enjoyed the humiliations and dangers of this lofty and tyrannic power, fhe may at length take arms in its defence. Should it be fo, the Courts of Verfailles and Madrid would fee themfelves fallen from the hope which they have conceived of a decifive preponderance upon the globe. Thefe confiderations fhould determine them to haften their attacks, and not give time, for the forming of new difpofitions, to a prophetic or even a jealous policy. Above all, let them ftop in time, and not fuffer an immoderate defire of humbling their common enemy to make them blind to their own interefts.

The United States have fhewn openly the project of drawing all North America to their league. Many meafures, that in particular of inviting the people of Canada to rebellion, have given caufe to believe that this was likewife the wifh of France. Spain may be fufpected to have equally adopted this idea.

M 4   The

The conduct of the provinces which have fhaken off the yoke of Great Britain is fimple, and fuch as was to be expected. But would not their allies be wanting in forefight, if they fhould have really the fame fyftem?

The new hemifphere muft be detached one day from the old. This grand fciffure is prepared in Europe, by the collifion and fermentation of our opinions; by our being deprived of our rights, which conftituted our courage; by the luxury of our courts and the mifery of our countries; by the hatred, the endlefs hatred, between men without heart, honour, or vigour, who poffefs all elfe, and robuft men, and even virtuous men, who have nothing but life to lofe. It is prepared in America, by the increafe of population, of cultivation, of induftry, and of knowledge. Every thing forwards this rupture, as well the progrefs of evil in the old world, as in the new the progrefs of good.

But would it be right for Spain and France, whofe poffeffions in the new world are an inexhauftible fource of riches, would

it

it be right for them to precipitate this rupture? Now this rupture is the thing that would precisely happen, were all the north of those regions subjected to the same laws, or bound together by a common interest.

No sooner would the liberty of this vast continent be established, than it would become the asylum, of all the offscouring amongst us, of men of intriguing, seditious spirits, blasted characters, or ruined fortunes. Culture, arts, commerce, would have no charms for such refugees as these. They must have a less laborious and more agitated life. This turn of mind, equally distant from labour or repose, would direct itself towards conquests; and a passion which has so many attractions would easily captivate the first colonists, diverted by a long war from their accustomed occupations. The new people would have compleated their preparations for invasion before the report of it had reached our climates. They would chuse their enemy, the field and the moment of their victories. Their thunder would fall always
upon

upon feas without defence, or on coafts taken at unawares. In a little while the Southern provinces would become their prey, and fupply by the riches of their productions the mediocrity of thofe of the Northern. Perhaps the poffeffions of our abfolute monarchies might even be candidates for the honour of being admitted to a confederacy with a free people, or would detach themfelves from Europe in order to belong but to themfelves.

The part which the Courts of Madrid and Verfailles fhould take, if they are free to chufe, is to let two powers fubfift in North America, who may watch, reftrain, and counterpoize each other. Then will ages roll away, before England and the republics formed at her expence can come together. This reciprocal diftruft will prohibit them from any diftant enterprize; and the eftablifhments, belonging to other nations, in the new world, will enjoy without difturbance that tranquillity, which, even down to our own times, has been fo often troubled.

In

In all probability, indeed, it is the very order of things which would be moft fuitable even for the confederate provinces themfelves. Their refpective limits are not regulated. A great jealoufy fubfifts between the countries to the northward and thofe to the fouthward. Political principles vary from one river to another. Great animofities are obferved between the inhabitants of the fame town, between the members of the fame family. Each would throw off from himfelf the heavy burden of public expences and debts. A thoufand principles of divifion are generally fpringing in the bofom of the United States. When dangers are once at an end, how is the explofion of fo many difcontents to be retarded? how are fo many unfettled minds, and angered hearts, to be held attached to a common centre? Let the true friends of America reflect upon it, and they will find that the only means to prevent difturbances, amongft that people, is to leave remaining on their frontiers a powerful rival, always difpofed to profit by their diffenfions.

Monar-

Monarchies thrive beft with peace and
fecurity; inquietudes, and formidable enemies, make republics flourifh. Rome had
need of Carthage; and he who deftroyed
the Roman liberty was neither Sylla, nor
Cæfar; it was the firft Cato, when his narrow and auftere politics took her rival away
from Rome, by lighting, in the fenate,
thofe torches which burnt Carthage to the
ground. Even Venice, perhaps, would
not have had her government, and her
laws, thefe four hundred years, had fhe
not had at her door powerful neighbours,
who might become her enemies or her
mafters.

What idea should be formed of the thirteen united pro- vinces.

But, fuppofing them thus fituated, to
what degree of happinefs, fplendour, and
power, may the united provinces in time
be raifed?

Here, in order to form a found judgement, let us immediately begin with laying afide the intereft which all hearts, not
excepting thofe of flaves, have taken in
the generous efforts of a people who expofed themfelves to the moft dreadful calamities to be free. The name of liberty
is

3

is fo fweet, that all they who fight for it
are fure to intereft our fecret wifhes. Their
caufe is that of the whole human race ; it
becomes our own. We revenge ourfelves
of our own oppreffors, by giving vent, at
leaft, with liberty, to our hatred againft
thofe oppreffors who cannot punifh it. At
the found of breaking chains, it feems as
if our own were about to become lighter ;
and we think for fome moments that we
breathe a purer air, in learning that fewer
tyrants are to be counted in the world.
Thefe great revolutions of liberty, moreover, admonifh defpots. They warn them
not to truft to too long patience in the people, not to truft to impunity without end.
Thus, when the laws of fociety execute
vengeance upon the crimes of private individuals, the good man hopes that the
punifhment of the guilty will, by its terrible example, prevent the commiffion of
new crimes. Terror fometimes fupplies
the place of juftice to the thief, and confcience to the affaffin. Such is the fource
of the warm intereft we feel in all the wars
of liberty Such is that with which we
have

have been infpired for the Americans. Our
imaginations have been inflamed in their
favour. We feem to be prefent at, and to
feel as they do, all their victories and their
defeats. The fpirit of juftice, which is
pleafed in compenfating paft mifery by
happinefs to come, is pleafed in thinking
that this part of the new world cannot fail
of becoming one of the moft flourifhing
countries upon the globe. Nay, it has
been even fuppofed, that there is caufe to
fear left Europe fhould one day find her
mafters in her children. Let us dare to
ftem the torrent of public opinion, and
that of public enthufiafm. Let us not be
led aftray by imagination, that embellifher
of all things, nor by paffion, which loves
to create illufions, and realizes all it hopes
Our duty is to combat every prejudice,
fhould it be even that which is moft con-
formable to the wifhes of our heart. To
be true, above all things, is our chief con
cern, and not to betray the pure and upright confcience which prefides over our
writings, and dictates every judgement
that we pafs. At this moment, perhaps,

we fhall not be believed : but a bold conjecture, which is verified at the end of
many ages, does more honour to the hiftorian, than the recital of a long feries of
facts which cannot be contefted; and I
write not only for my contemporaries, who
will but fome years furvive me. Yet a
few revolutions of the fun, and they and I
fhall be no more. But I deliver over my
ideas to pofterity and to time. It is for
them to judge me.

The fpace occupied by the thirteen republics, between the mountains and the
ocean, is but of fixty-feven fea-leagues;
but upon the coaft-their extent is, in a
ftrait line, three hundred and forty-five.

In this region the lands are, almoft
throughout, bad, or of a middling quality. Scarcely any thing but maize grows
in the four moft northern colonies. The
only refource of their inhabitants is fifhery,
of which the annual product, in money,
does not amount to above two hundred and
fixty or feventy thoufand pounds.

Corn fuftains principally the provinces of
New York, Jerfey, and Pennfylvania. But
the

the foil there is fo rapidly become worfe than it was, that an acre, which formerly yielded full fixty bufhels of wheat, now produces but very rarely above twenty.

Though the foil of Maryland and Virginia is much fuperior to all the reft, it cannot be faid to be very fruitful. The old plantations do not yield above a third of the tobacco which they formerly produced. It is not poffible to form new ones; and the cultivators have been obliged to turn their views towards other objects.

North Carolina produces fome corn, but of a quality fo inferior, that it is fold for five and twenty, or thirty per cent. lefs than the other, in all the markets.

South Carolina and Georgia have a perfectly flat face of country, for the diftance of fifty miles from the fea-fide. The exceffive rains which fall there, finding no means of difcharge, form numerous marfhes or lakes, in which rice is cultivated, to the great detriment of the flaves and the freemen occupied in this labour. On the intermediate fpaces left by thefe multitudinous

nous little feas, grows an inferior kind of indigo, which muſt have its place changed every year. Where the country riſes from the level, it is but with ungrateful ſands or frightful rocks, interſperſed, from diſtance to diſtance, with paſtures of the nature of ruſh.

The Engliſh government, ſeeing that North America could never enrich them by the productions proper to that country, thought of the powerful motive of premiums, for the creating in this part of the new world, of linen, wine, and ſilk. The poverty of the ſoil, which would not bear flax, obſtructed the firſt of theſe views ; the badneſs of the climate, which would not agree with vines, oppoſed the ſucceſs of the ſecond ; and the want of hands permitted not the third to take place. The ſociety eſtabliſhed at London, for the encouragement of arts, manufactures and commerce, was not more happy than the miniſtry had been. It's premiums did not give birth to any one of the objects which it had propoſed to the activity and induſtry of thoſe countries.

N   Great

Great Britain was obliged to content herfelf with felling every year to thefe countries, merchandize to the amount of fomething more than two millions. The confumers of this merchandize delivered up to her, exclufively, their indigo, their iron, their tobacco, and their furs. They delivered up to her whatever money, and raw materials, the reft of the globe had given them for their wood, their corn, their fifh, their rice, and their falted provifions. Yet the balance was always fo much againft them, that, when the troubles began, the colonies owed from five to fix millions to the mother-country, and had no cafh in circulation.

Notwithftanding thefe difadvantages, there had been fucceffively formed, within the thirteen provinces, a population of two millions nine hundred eighty-one thoufand fix hundred and feventy-eight perfons, including four hundred thoufand negroes. Oppreffion and intolerance were continually driving thither new inhabitants. The war has now barred this refuge to the unhappy; but the peace will open it to them again;

4   when

when they will flock thither in greater
numbers than ever. They who fhall go
with projects of cultivation will not have
all the fatisfaction which they may promife
themfelves, becaufe they will find the good
land, and even the middling, all occupied;
and there will be nothing to be offered them
but barren fands, unhealthy marfhes, or
fteep mountains. Emigration will be more
favourable to manufacturers and artifts,
tho' even they may, perhaps, gain nothing
by their change of country and climate.

We cannot determine, without rafhnefs, what may one day be the population
of the United States. Such a calculation,
generally pretty difficult, becomes imprac-
ticable for a region where the land dege-
nerates very rapidly, and where the expence of labour and improvement is not
proportionably anfwered by the reproduc-
tion. If ten millions of men ever find a
certain fubfiftence in thefe provinces, it
will be much. Even then the exportation
will be reduced to nothing, or next to
nothing : but interior induftry will replace
foreign induftry. The country, within a

N 2   little,

little, will be able to fuffice for itfelf, provided that the inhabitants know how to make themfelves happy by œconomy and with mediocrity.

Ye people of North America, let the example of all the nations who have gone before you, and above all that of your mother-country, ferve you for inftruction. Fear the affluence of gold, which brings with luxury the corruption of manners, the contempt of laws. Fear a too unequal diftribution of riches, which exhibits a fmall number of citizens in opulence, and a great multitude of citizens in extreme poverty; whence fprings the infolence of the former, and the debafement of the latter. Secure yourfelves againft the fpirit of conqueft. The tranquillity of an empire diminifhes in proportion to its extenfion. Have arms for your defence; have none for offence. Seek competency and health in labour; profperity in the culture of lands, and the workfhops of induftry; power in manners and virtue. Caufe arts and fciences, which diftinguifh the civilifed from the favage man, to flourifh and abound.

Above

Above all, watch carefully over the education of your children. It is from public fchools, be affured, that come the wife magiftrates, the capable and courageous foldiers, the good fathers, the good hufbands, the good brothers, the good friends, the good men. Wherever the youth are feen depraved, the nation is on the decline. Let liberty have an immoveable foundation in the wifdom of your laws, and let it be the indeftructible cement to bind your provinces together. Eftablifh no legal preference amongft the different forms of worfhip. Superftition is innocent, wherever it is neither perfecuted nor protected; and may your duration, if it be poffible, equal the duration of the world!

F I N I S.

For EU product safety concerns, contact us at Calle de José Abascal, 56–1°, 28003 Madrid, Spain or eugpsr@cambridge.org.

www.ingramcontent.com/pod-product-compliance
Ingram Content Group UK Ltd.
Pitfield, Milton Keynes, MK11 3LW, UK
UKHW012345130625
459647UK00009B/537